making
hope

making
hope

Practices, Prayers, and Parables
for a Changing Climate

o'neil van horn

ORBIS BOOKS
Maryknoll, New York 10545

Founded in 1970, Orbis Books endeavors to publish works that enlighten the mind, nourish the spirit, and challenge the conscience. The publishing arm of the Maryknoll Fathers and Brothers, Orbis seeks to explore the global dimensions of the Christian faith and mission, to invite dialogue with diverse cultures and religious traditions, and to serve the cause of reconciliation and peace. The books published reflect the views of their authors and do not represent the official position of the Maryknoll Society. To learn more about Maryknoll and Orbis Books, please visit our website at www.orbisbooks.com.

Copyright © 2026 by O'neil Van Horn
Published by Orbis Books, Box 302, Maryknoll, NY 10545-0302.
All rights reserved.
Scripture quotations, unless otherwise noted, are from New Revised Standard Version Bible: Catholic Edition, copyright © 1989, 1993 National Council of the Churches of Christ in the United States of America. Used by permission. All rights reserved worldwide.

Queries regarding rights and permissions should be addressed to: Orbis Books, P.O. Box 302, Maryknoll, NY 10545-0302.

Manufactured in the United States of America

Library of Congress Cataloging-in-Publication Data

Names: Van Horn, O'neil, author.
Title: Making hope : practices, prayers, and parables for a changing climate / O'neil Van Horn.
Description: Maryknoll, NY : Orbis Books, [2026] | Includes bibliographical references and index. | Summary: "Practicing hope in ways that promote environmental justice and well-being"—Provided by publisher.
Identifiers: LCCN 2025019759 (print) | LCCN 2025019760 (ebook) | ISBN 9781626986404 (trade paperback) | ISBN 9798888660959 (epub)
Subjects: LCSH: Hope—Religious aspects—Christianity. | Environmental justice—Religious aspects—Christianity. | Well-being—Religious aspects—Christianity.
Classification: LCC BV4638 .V364 2026 (print) | LCC BV4638 (ebook)
LC record available at https://lccn.loc.gov/2025019759
LC ebook record available at https://lccn.loc.gov/2025019760

Contents

For those who sow and tend.
And for all who resist in love.

Acknowledgments

For the many companions who have walked alongside, nourished, affirmed, humbled, and cared for me in this season, I am unspeakably thankful. This book would not exist but for the beautiful and awesome multispecies community in which I am enmeshed. There are many—named and unnamed—who have held me through this work.

Specifically, I am grateful to:

My students—with their ravenous and wild curiosity—for teaching me more than they know.

My colleagues for steadying me amid turbulent times: Kathleen Smythe for her earnest wisdom and relentless joy, not to mention crucial comments on early drafts; Elliott Chen and Alexis Dianda for their comradeship and especially their conversation as this project was just beginning to take shape; Kristen Renzi for her sharp eye and incisive wit, shepherding this manuscript and its author in many ways.

My dear friends for their unyielding care and courageous witness, not to mention whimsy: Meredith Irwin and John Klingler for their adventurous passion for foraging; Matt Latchaw for his reliable presence; Lyric Morris-Latchaw for her creative spirit and reminder to practice sacred remembering; Chris La Rue for his grounding support; Nathan Mather for his insightful mind and cheerful demeanor; Jen Murray for generously sharing her mending expertise with my students; Alyssa Overkamp for her warmth and hospitality; Sam Overkamp for his deep friendship and unmistakable mirth; Jacob Taylor for his theological vision, aflame.

The little ones in my life who inspire the child within me: Maeve, Rory, Damian, Meadow, June, Ayla Mae, and more for their sheer gladness.

My teachers—of whom there are many, but especially: Catherine Keller for her theological imagination and irreplaceable guidance; Laurel Kearns for her tenacious advocacy and enduring mentorship; Jeff Markay for his quiet reassurance and joy for cosmic coffee.

The people who kept me fed in both body and spirit: Robert Lockridge and Erin Tuttle-Lockridge for their deep commitment to making hope in our neighborhood; the farmers at the Community Supported Garden at Genesis Farm—not least Judith "Judy" von Handorf—for modeling the steadfastness needed for living in a climate-changed world; Karen and Tom Wuest for their earnest welcome, depth of character, and incessant reminder to "get lost" and "figure out where you are."

My collaborators on this project: Tess Dankoski for her inspired work on rewilding and her keen attention to detail for this book's index; the inestimable Tom Hermans-Webster for his editing expertise and now jubilant friendship; Megan Suttman for her exemplary practice of making hope through art and liturgy, and especially for the artwork that is now the cover of this book.

My family for their unrivaled support of my work—in all its weirdness—and their love, which means more than they could imagine.

My partner, Jen, without whom nothing I do would be possible. I owe her the world.

Opening

Hope Doesn't Exist

I might as well be honest with you: Hope doesn't exist. I figured I should just get that out of the way at the outset.

There's no such thing as hope. There's no reason we should have hope. Or, really, what I actually mean to say is that there's no way we *can have* hope.

That's all a little dramatic, I know, but I do mean it—just maybe not in the way one might assume.

So why talk about hope? Or why write a book with that very word in the title for that matter? Before you throw this book across whatever space you find yourself in, let me clarify.

I really don't think there's such a "*thing*" as hope. Nor do I think that it's some*thing* we can "have." Hope is not a "thing." And it's not something to be "had."

Hope is not something we have
so much as something we make.

Hope is a doing, a partnering, a communing, a creating, a crafting. It's active and animating; it demands something of us. It's not a noun but a verb. It's not an object; it's a force.

Anything less than this and hope simply leads to apathy, to passivity, to inaction. Anything less and hope is just a carrot dangled on a string. It tempts and tantalizes but does not liberate us from the cart's yoke. And what's hopeful about any of that? A hope that isn't catalyzing or motivating *isn't hope at all.*

As theologian Willie J. Jennings puts it, "Hope is a discipline."[1] Or, as he states rather forcefully, "We have to be disciplined by hope."[2]

Hope is a habit. It is praxis; and, thus, it's something we must *learn* to practice. We cannot have hope, as though it were an entity or domain for our own gain or manipulation, but we can co-create it by partnering with the world around us. Thus, as Palestinian liberation theologian Mitri Raheb argues, "Hope is what we do today."[3]

Hope is an orientation, a way-making, a laboring. Hence this is not a book that will teach you how to "have" hope. That's not the goal, and I wouldn't be the person to do that even if I thought it were possible. Rather, this book intends to help us learn *how to make hope.*

We must *apprentice* ourselves to hope.

☙

What Is This Book Even About?

So, what exactly are you reading then? How does this book intend to discuss this whole hope business? And what is this book that breaks the fourth wall so candidly—if inappropriately?

This is a book of practices, prayers, and parables about weaving hope in a world that, by all accounts, seems to be unraveling quickly. To state it plainly, this book is about two things:

First, it's a book about stories. Not just a book "of" stories—yes, there are those—but a book *about* the stories we tell. Or stories we've been told, anyway. This is a book that questions the principles of our many societal narratives—such as what they instill in us, how they instruct us to live, why they're so powerful, and so on.

And, second, it's a book about the hope that various slow, quiet practices can cultivate. It's a book about how the things we do—like sewing and fixing and patching and planting—can reshape our stories and help us prayerfully *make hope*. It's a book about *learning from doing*. These practices can help us reimagine the larger stories our communities tell. These practices, as will become apparent, can serve as parables for a planet in distress.

Why? Or what does this even mean? What stories need to be reimagined anyway?

cℐ

Stories Are Everywhere

Everything tells a story, and everything is storied. Our variously intersecting crises—climate catastrophe, white supremacy, heterosexism, transphobia, and fascism, to name a few—are motivated by some particularly bad stories.

Take climate change as an example: One of the principal drivers of climate change is the story of capitalism. Capitalism's story is rather simple and very bad. We can tell it in a variety of ways, though it seems to cause uncountable forms of harm no matter how we tell it.

Here are a few versions of it: Capitalism is a story that tells us to profit as much as possible, whenever possible, however possible. Or, it's a story about *infinite growth*, necessitating *infinite extraction*, on a planet with *finite resources*. Or, it's a story that values something only so long as it's useful or *instrumental*, and it couldn't care less about the possibility that things can have *intrinsic* value: trees are valuable only insofar as they can become lumber, cows are valuable only insofar as they can become beef, you're valuable only insofar as you can be productive and efficient (usually on somebody else's behalf and for somebody else's benefit), and so on. No matter how you tell it, capitalism's a pretty bad story.

If you are unconvinced, I invite you to ask yourself and be honest with yourself about your responses:

- Is capitalism capable of thinking of the world as *anything other than* commodities, objects, or things? Can capitalism tell any other story?
- According to capitalism, do you or I have any *intrinsic* value whatsoever?
- What *moral* framework guides capitalism?
- What *ensures* that capitalism will realize goodness or compassion or justice or equity?

If capitalism can only see the world as commodities, as objects, as things, then there's no way it will ever be capable of slowing, much less reversing, climate catastrophe. The climatic catastrophes we face are inextricable from the story of capitalism. They're the *inevitable consequence* of this story.

Climate change will persist as long as capitalism remains alive and well. This is because capitalism only pursues that which produces profit, and things like compassion or justice or equity are rarely profitable. And even when they are profitable, is pursuing these things merely for profit a good or ethical thing? Hardly.

A system predicated on profit—or, if we really want to be cynical, exploitation, which is but a synonym for profit—cannot ensure the creation of good communities, much less thriving ecosystems or healthy watersheds. Capitalism is an objectifying, materialistic, and incredibly forceful story. It's prevalent not because it's popular so much as it is potent.

I suggest that, so long as we tell the story of capitalism, keeping it alive in our practices and continuing to be suffused by its ideologies, climate injustice will persist. I am inspired by the Red Nation, an indigenous environmental justice collective, on this: "What creates crisis cannot solve it!"[4]

So how might we tell a different story? And what sorts of hopeful disciplines will help us reimagine the current damaging stories that poison the waters in which we swim?

While this book doesn't intend to explicitly theorize an alternative economic paradigm (many other books do this far better than I ever could[5]), it does suggest that other sensibilities can be—and, in fact, *are*—cultivated by things like mending, baking, and foraging. These alternative sensibilities can help us re-story how we define value, worth, success, goodness, and so on. This book seeks to uncover the parables that these practices have to teach us so that we might undo the potent narratives underlying many present injustices.

Simply put, this is a book about the restoration—or, the mending of the world—that can only come by way of "re-story-ation," as agricultural ecologist Gary Nabhan calls it.[6] How we think about the world shapes the practices we undertake, and those practices then come to shape how we think about the world. Stories shape practices; practices shape stories. It's cyclical and reciprocal. It can become a vicious feedback loop or, as seems more often the case, a death spiral. Or this flowing cycle can be wholesome and compassionate. We have some choice in the matter.

This book asks a lot of questions about the current stories we tell and what alternatives might be possible. For example,

- How might the practice of seed-saving reshape our relationship to our bioregions?
- What might fermentation have to teach us about communing with others?
- How might birding help us come to experience the world anew?
- How might these activities help us cultivate new lifeways for the sake of a hope-full world? And how might they reshape our perceptions of the good, holy, and sacred on this planet?

ℭ

On Practices

This book traces the threads of a variety of practices, each of which discloses a lesson to instruct us to better inhabit a world whose climate has changed and, it seems, will continue to change—likely drastically. We are indeed at the precipice of what appears to be the sixth mass extinction event on this planet.[7] The speed of peril does not seem to be slowing anytime soon.

It is tempting to respond to the rapidity of climate change with *speed*. Yes, the need to respond *quickly* to this pending global catastrophe is obvious. But, perhaps paradoxically, this book intends to make a case for the value of *slowing down*—that is, embracing slowness as the paradoxical antidote to hasty problems.

We cannot care for that which we've yet to notice, and we can only notice by reorienting our senses and slowing down. Slowness might yet enable survival. To this end, this book focuses on practices of slowness as well as survival.

The practices that are featured here might aid in our survival, but they're also included here because they function as a vector for other possible lifeways. These practices might enable survival, but they also do the crucial work of stimulating our imagination. Put differently, the practices that I'm interested in and that are explored in this book are ones that remind us that *another way is possible*.

These practices help us *imagine the world otherwise*. Indeed, the world must be imagined otherwise, and imagining it otherwise is the habit of hope.

These practices are meant to catalyze paradigm shifts in both our thought and action, our theory and praxis. These practices are *material* and *symbolic*: They matter—as in, they effect meaningful change in the world, in my opinion—but they also symbolize alternative modes of living beyond each practice's immediate concerns. They are good in themselves but are also good insofar as they serve as models for other ways of life.

But how exactly are these practices symbolic?

To give a sense of what I mean, let's use the example of mending, the subject of a later chapter. Mending teaches us to care for our things—clothes, especially. The practice sustains goods, creates beauty, and resists consumerism. Mending is good in and of itself.

What's more, mending *also* has the capacity, I will argue, to help us rethink how we conceive of justice, equity, history, memory, and more. Mending is about fixing clothes, but it can also serve as a symbol for *so much more*. Mending serves as a model to help us reimagine the world and our place in it, helping us understand how to better respond to interpersonal and societal trauma, for example.

Each chapter in this book focuses on practices themselves and on the stories they tell: that is, the parables they offer for prayerful ways of living on this shifting planet.

Thus, the discussions of various practices that emerge in the subsequent chapters are material *and* metaphoric. I'm hoping that they offer us opportunities to learn not only about those (material) skills and why they're good but, further, how those skills can (metaphorically) translate into broader social movements and communal efforts to realize wholesomeness—or, in a word, shalom.

෴

On Parables

Parables are a genre of storytelling. They're often associated with Christianity and, more specifically, with Jesus of Nazareth. The genre of parables is not unique to Jesus, though his parables are certainly unique.

The four canonical Gospels of the Christian New Testament (known generally as Matthew, Mark, Luke, and John) each feature stories about and told by the storytelling man whom today we call Jesus. The parables Jesus tells are critical to the larger stories we call the Gospels. But I think they're often misunderstood. That is, I think that the genre of the parable itself is misunderstood.

Parables are symbolic narratives that intend to communicate some sort of teaching, lesson, or moral. That's simple enough, I think, but I want to challenge two common assumptions about parables by making the following two arguments: first, there is no "one true meaning" to any given parable; second, parables, as biblical scholar William R. Herzog II put it, are "not earthly stories with heavenly meanings but earthly stories with *heavy* meanings."[8]

Making Meaning

Parables are not divine puzzles with a single meaning that we can access with enough prayer, study, revelation, or the like. We don't ever arrive at one true meaning of a parable for all times, places, and peoples. Parables are not singular: they're cloudy, amorphous, malleable. They're not straightforward, *and they're not meant to be straightforward.* That's not the point of them at all!

Parables are an invitation into dialogue. They open up space for debate.

Think about how Jesus uses parables in the context of the Gospels. One great example comes from a well-known parable about a supposedly "good" Samaritan.[9] We turn to the content of this parable in just a moment, but first, let's just look at the context in which Jesus seems to tell this story. (If you're unfamiliar with the story and its context, take a minute to look it up and read it in Luke 10:25–37.)

As Luke tells it, Jesus is speaking with a lawyer—an expert on the law and a member of the political elite. Testing Jesus on the commandments, the lawyer asks him what he must do "to inherit eternal life." Jesus provides the orthodox answer expected of him: "You shall love the Lord your God with all your heart and with all your soul and with all your strength and with all your mind and your neighbor as yourself." But the lawyer continues to press Jesus, asking, "And who is my neighbor?" Jesus could have responded to this question in a simple, straightforward way. Yet, in typical Jesus fashion, he doesn't. Instead, he tells a story, "A man was going down from Jerusalem to Jericho. . . ."

This story does something that no straightforward response could ever do: it sparks conversation and creates community. The listeners are left to mull over a metaphoric tale about very material realities. The story is an invitation *into the way* that Jesus seems to be sharing—not a "new religion" but rather an effort to imagine the world otherwise, here and now.

This is reflected in how the story about Jesus's parable resolves: Having finished his tale, Jesus mirrors the question asked of him back at the lawyer: "Which of these three, do you think, was a neighbor to the man who fell into the hands of the robbers?" Jesus invites the lawyer into a renewed vision of the world, and the lawyer rightly responds, "The one who showed him mercy." The lesson comes by means not of imposition but of invitation!

Consider the impact that this story left. Imagine the murmurings that passed through the crowd of listeners: "Wait, who is *my* neighbor?" "Do you think he really means that —— are our neighbors?" "How am I supposed to live *that* way?" "What would it look like for me to show mercy as did the Samaritan?" "Do I *even want* to live that way?"

Notice that not only does this teaching happen by means of invitation, but the invitation is one that is ongoing, open-ended, on the way. There is no one singular way of being a good neighbor, just as there is no one singular way of showing mercy. The invitation is, thus, to find opportunities for mercy in each present moment. We never arrive at being a good neighbor; we can only ever continue to practice good neighborliness—now, and now, and now, and. . . .

The point of parables is that they resist oneness, finality, and certainty. They invite us into a new way of being. And because of this, *their wisdom is not found on the page.* Rather, their wisdom can only be found in communal conversation and spirited debate! They do not have meaning intrinsically, but they are *made meaningful* in our embodiment of their spirit.

If we never arrive at a final answer from a parable, that's because there never was one. The great gift that parables offer is that they utilize symbols, allowing them to remain relevant in a shifting and shaking world. They are alive—or, at the very least, are *enlivening*. They continue to teach us, if we have but ears to hear.

Heavenly Heavy Meanings

Let's consider the *content* of the parable of the good Samaritan, noting its social and material dimensions. The parable takes on greater meaning when we consider the characters of the parable and their social locations (i.e., their race, class, religious identity, and so forth). Doing so uncovers some of the heavy valences that would have been obvious to the initial hearers of this story but are perhaps obscured to the contemporary reader, given the vast time and cultural differences separating us from the world behind the text.

We must first ask: Who were the Samaritans? And why might this matter?

Suffice it to say that the Samaritans were despised by the audience with whom Jesus spoke.[10] Despite their relative religious and cultural similarities,[11] Jesus's Jewish audience would have likely detested Samaritans. Thus, any story featuring a Samaritan in this context would have typically cast them as an antagonist. Even the phrase "good Samaritan" would have been understood as an oxymoron and a contradiction of terms (though, for the record, this phrase never actually appears in Luke's Gospel).

In the typically atypical fashion of this parabler called Jesus, the script is flipped: the last become first and the first last. The likeliest good-doer—the Levite, according to the audience's assumptions, given that they are aligned with his tradition—neglects his responsibility to "the least of these. The unlikeliest good-doer—the Samaritan, the "other," the outsider, the enemy—demonstrates neighborliness in no uncertain terms. And the person assumed to be holiest by "the establishment" was not only a bad neighbor: he was no neighbor at all!

It's apparent that discriminatory worldviews and marginalizing deeds—whether intentional or not—have no place in the kin(g)dom of God. The Levite's responsibilities to religious dogmatism do not supersede the acts of lovingkindness needed by the robbed and beaten man in the ditch. The radical nature of the Way that the parabler invites his audience into can be summed thusly: love of God and love of neighbor are interconnected. To love one's neighbor is to love God, and we cannot love God if we do not love our neighbor.[12] These are not separate commandments, Jesus suggests to the audience. They're entangled.

This is a story with a heavy—not heavenly—meaning. By that, I mean that this story has consequences for our world here-now and not merely for some flight into a cloudy afterlife. The intention here is thus to remind that heavenliness can be and *ought to be* found among us. This is precisely why it seems that the Samaritan *had to be* a Samaritan in this tale: the story would have meant little if the Samaritan were any other person or were left anonymous. The social location of the Samaritan as a marginalized and detested person discloses that anyone desiring to be a good neighbor is obligated to not just be a charitable giver but to create communities that are not characterized by intolerance, injustice, or oppression in the first place.

The ethics of this parabler concerns our love for not just "any" neighbor but—specifically and *especially*—the social outcast in our midst. Hence the whole "first shall be last and the last shall be first" business: perhaps it is the case that the beloved community illustrated by Jesus is not merely a reversal of existing hierarchies but rather a world in which there can be no hierarchies, no relationships marked by coercive power, to begin with![13] This *kin*dom is constituted by horizontal relations of compassion rather than vertical associations of dominance. Hierarchies crumble when we create truly good and neighborly communities. Until then, it seems that the divine is to be found at the margins, among the "least of these."

Feel free, then, to translate this story for the time and place in which you presently read this book. In the present moment of this author's context, the Levite would perhaps be a white evangelical megachurch pastor and the Samaritan an undocumented Black trans woman.

Notice, then, that the parable invites, indeed implicates, the contemporary reader for the here-and-now in some heavy ways: we are forced to question our assumptions, to challenge the status quo, and to deconstruct the divisions that separate us—from one another and from the divine, at once.

This book approaches the contemporary parables illustrated by each chapter's specific practice in a similar fashion. That is, the stories taught to us by the sense-reorienting practices included here offer *heavy* meanings for our present—*in order to make our present more heavenly.*

⁓

On Prayer

What exactly is prayer?

Our conceptualization of what "prayer" means can often be limited to an eyes-closed, head-bowed, hands-clasped muttering. It's a private thing. It's subdued. This is fine, but it's also a bit narrow.

Why not expand our definition of prayer? What if we were to toss aside these conventional notions and postures of prayer for a moment? What alternative, reimagined conceptualizations might emerge?

Poet Mary Oliver is honest with readers in her poem "The Summer Day."[14] In it, she confesses that she doesn't quite know what a prayer is. Yet, in her honest unknowing and humble admission, she notes that she does know how to *pay attention,* how to be *utterly and thoroughly present,* how to *appreciate the intricacies* of the world around her. Despite not knowing what "prayer" is, the poet asks, is there something else that she ought to do? What more is there for the narrator to do than embrace the present goodness about her and cultivate a compassionate attention to creatures and landscapes about her—perhaps even that which has given life to her environs?

What else should she be doing? Isn't this precisely what prayer *is*? Or *ought to be,* anyway? Becoming drawn into the presence of the mysteries that often elude us?

The poem concludes with a striking inquiry: "What do you plan to do with your one and only life?"

As a professor of theology at a Jesuit university, my classes are often required courses. This means that I have students who occupy a broad spectrum of religious affiliations, curiosities, and traumas—all of whom are *required* to be in my classes regardless of whether they'd like to be. My students run the gamut from ultraconservative, observant Catholics to militantly outspoken atheists. It's a fun and often dicey challenge to address the concerns and needs of this array of students. I have to assuage some that I'm not there to "convert" them and remind others that my job is not to affirm all of their theological convictions. Rather, I tell them—and have to remind them weekly—that my job is to create opportunities for them to engage the big human questions that theology deals with, to address contemporary ethical issues, and to learn to build community with one another in spite of their differences. In other words, our task is to learn to ask better questions—questions that will foster love, compassion, and justice in and for our world.

For this reason, I read Mary Oliver's "The Summer Day" to my students every semester on the very first day of class. In fact, they are some of the first words they hear me utter, as I usually open the class with this poem. It is, if only subtly, my prayer for the students and the semester ahead.

But, truthfully, I read it because my hope is that Oliver's questions will spark something in them: What *am* I doing with my precious and only life? What am I doing here at college? And not just here at college but here on Earth? What does it mean to live purposefully? To live *prayerfully*?

These questions matter to them—and hopefully to you, in some respect—regardless of religious identity or background. All of these questions are fundamentally theological questions. I read this poem to my students to begin to convince them that theology, broadly, and prayer, specifically, are not separate from life but are fundamentally about *how we live*.

> *Theology is nothing if it's not lived;*
> *prayer is nothing if it's not embodied.*

Prayer is not apart from our lives but is, I think, the very substance of our lives. We pray through our actions, and our actions are prayers—good or ill—in the midst of a troublesome world.

This book intends to explore prayer through action by asking questions like these: What would it look like to *live prayerfully*? For prayer to be active and public—not preachy words shouted on a street corner but *embodied in our habits and disciplines?* What, then, is the work of prayer?

∽

On Practices, Prayers, and Parables

What I hope is becoming apparent is that the phenomena of practices, prayers, and parables are not separable. They're entangled. They mix and mingle.

Prayer is the embodiment of faithful *practice*. Practices are the compassionate habits formed by *parables*. Parables are the *prayerful* inspiration of the world imagined otherwise. And on . . .

Over the course of this book, I will speak of these things individually at times, but they are never actually so. Each is an outgrowth of the other, but trying to trace their individual contours helps us notice the threads of each one's contributions to making hope in a climate-changed world.

☙

Context Matters

I've only ever experienced the world as me. You've only experienced it as you. And our experiences of the world are influenced and affected by our various positionalities—how we present, what we wear, which pronouns we use, how we speak, what language(s) we speak, what our abilities are, how we identify religiously, what resources we have access to, and so on.

How the world perceives me influences my experiences of it. And because I've only ever experienced it as me, sometimes I'm tempted to assume that others' experiences of the world are similar—that we share values, cultural cues, perceptions, and the like. Of course, this couldn't be further from the case. My life as a cisgender, white, masculine, able-bodied person is markedly different from those whose social locations differ from my own. Even those who share these same descriptors but, say, grew up in a rural Appalachian holler as opposed to the dusty coastal hills of Southern California (where I was raised) still would have a substantively different experience. These differences of identity, culture, and experience are what make the world beautiful and also complicated.

I note this at the outset because I intend to offer a book that's helpful to others while also being mindful of the differences by which we're constituted. If I use the terms "we" or "us" over the course of this book, I only ever do so *invitationally*.

I don't mean to presume that we share the same experiences or worldview. Perhaps there's something of my experience that connects with something of yours. Lovely. Perhaps our experiences diverge. Lovely, all the same. My aim here is not to convince you of anything, per se. I write this book as an invitation to you into these practices, prayers, and parables as I have experienced them. This invitation does not demand your agreement with or affinity for any of these things. I simply invite you to be with them. To become with them. This book is my attempt to do the same.

∽

How to Read This Book

In our ever-quickening world, it's hard to pick up a book. The speed of our world does not lend itself to the slowness of reading. That's my experience, anyway. It's ironic, too, since I make my livelihood as a professor. You might assume that my world revolves around books. And that's true—it does in many ways, sure—but that doesn't make opening, much less reading, those books any easier. Even for me.

So, let me confess a few things:

I've never been much of a reader. Maybe the same is true for you. I find reading difficult because it forces me to be still with myself. I'm not particularly good at being still with myself because of the world where I've been socialized.

If you're anything like me, I think you'll agree with me on this: Being still with myself incites in me an urge to seek distraction. It's much easier to be distracted—by social media, by hobbies, or by really anything at all besides reading—than it is to face the big questions that arise when I do happen to quiet my mind. Being with myself, as musicians Phoebe Bridgers and Conor Oberst put it, means, "I have to listen to me think." I'm not very good at listening to me think.[15] (Listening to me talk is a separate thing that I love to do, but that's another matter entirely.) Listening requires being present, and that presence is often only the result of mindful diligence.

Cultivating this discipline is terribly hard in a world that generally prioritizes anything but being mindful. Reading requires a stillness that's often tough for me to muster. So, if any of this resonates with you, please know that *you are not alone*—whatsoever.

I share these confessions to say that reading is a difficult—indeed *courageous*—act.

Reading makes little sense in a world that prioritizes efficiency, speed, productivity, and other "values" meant to distract us from the violence those principles perpetuate—on humans, on Earth. To read requires a willingness to be still, to be present to oneself and to the text. It means working hard to inhabit the thought-world of the author. But somewhere deep within, I know—have always known—that reading is good *because* it is slow, because it demands stillness, and that practicing this sort of presence is a radical thing to do.

The fact that you're here, having opened this book and now reading these words, is not something I take lightly. The presence and stillness you practice here-now are important. Reading encourages us to inhabit a slower speed of life and a less distracted mindset. And these are the sorts of skills that are necessary for noticing the damage of a climate-changed world and responding compassionately to it. By reading, you are already beginning to practice some of what this book hopes to cultivate in both you and me.

Maybe these struggles hardly pertain to you. Maybe you've always been a reader and can't imagine life without a habit of reading regularly. Or maybe you're reading this because some professor like me mandated that you read it. Still—whoever you are, however you are—I remain grateful to you for your presence, curiosity, and diligence, regardless of what brings you here-now.

In any case, like most books, it probably makes sense to read the book in the order that it's presented to you here. It's organized in a way that makes sense to me—and hopefully to you, too.

Here's a brief outline, if helpful:

The first section, "Noticing," suggests the following: We cannot care for that which we have yet to notice. This first section focuses on practices of slowness, stillness, and presence as the grounds for hopeful world-mending. The chapters of this opening section intend to help us learn how slowing down might better enable us to make hope in the world by first cultivating our *prayerful attention.*

If the first section is about being drawn into mindful presence, then the second section, "Gathering," is about beginning to commune—across time, space, and species—with our planetary coinhabitants. This section asks: What are the practices, prayers, and parables that will help us form justice-seeking communities? How can we gather well and faithfully in tumultuous times?

The final section of the book, "Repairing," centers on opportunities for change-making. This section particularly emphasizes practices of world-mending. In other words, it explores several practices of repair that function as models for justice-seeking movements.

The organization of this book is an attempt to be liturgical, in a sense: drawing us into presence before our perilous planet and our experiences of the sacred in and among it, seeking lessons to help us create and sustain faithful communities, and then sending us forth with a renewed spirit to enact goodness.

But the book wasn't written in this order, of course. So you shouldn't feel bad if you skip around. I'm sure I would skip around.

Regardless, you'll find that each chapter experiments with narrative and poetics, and each concludes with some kind of embodied practice as a way to live out some of the chapter's arguments— should you be so inclined.

Please know then, dear reader, that I am writing this book to you as much as I am writing it to me. We're companions in this work together, sharing this precarious planet and its unknown future. And that's why this book is an attempt to *learn from* (not "teach about") various practices, prayers, and parables in an effort to reimagine "the good life" on this rapidly climatically changing planet. These practices, prayers, and parables are both the teachers and the lessons at once. I'm but their steward.

The future is always open-ended. The moral arc of the universe only bends toward justice if we toil to make it do so. And, given the uncertainties of the *particular* moment at which I write this to you now—mere days before the unthinkable second inauguration of Donald Trump—I can only pray that what you hold here will be a relevant and fruitful companion to you amid vast precarity. I know not what lies ahead, but I do know that the work of making hope will not become any less important than it has always been.

Noticing

Here

It's cold outside. Winter. Through the smudged front window of my home, I can see my mailman, bundled, across the street, delivering envelopes to my neighbors. I don't know why I'm writing this, really, or where I'm going. I simply know that I am here. *Here.* I am here. And this is *now.* And I am writing these words.

And you—whoever you are, someone, somewhere—are also here-now. Not with-me-here-now as I write these words. That would be weird. But you *are* here-now, in whatever configuration of space and time you happen to have this book before you, reading them.

Time is strange. My cat naps on her favorite chair near the front window—the one she's frustratingly territorial about, not allowing her feline sister anywhere near. My cat naps because she thinks of only the here-now. Or that's what I've learned from her and other cats I know, anyway. I don't mean to suggest that she's selfish, really. She *is* selfish with that chair, sure, but not all the time. My cat naps because she is fully here-now. My cat naps because, well, what else should she be doing? What else is there to do?

What else is there to do? Not what else is there to do but "nap"? But, rather, what else is there to do but to be thoroughly, wholly here-now? What other place or time is there but here-and-now? It's all there is.

So, I sit and write these words. They're not the most beautiful or poetic or even "deep" words. I'm not striving for that, and I'm not sure I'd be capable of that—at least not with how I'm feeling this morning. But they are words, and I am here. And you are here. Now. Alive. Present. And maybe a little bit cold. At least I am.

༝

On the Future

The future does not exist.

There's no such thing as "the future." There's not even "*a* future."

I don't mean that there's no hope for the future—that it's going to be miserable or something like that. Not in the least, though that's a possibility, I suppose. I mean that there is *no* "future." None. Period. It's not a thing. Does not exist. It's not out there, just waiting around until it can, after who knows how long, finally make an appearance. And it's not merely a mystery yet to make itself known to us or be revealed to us. It's simply—*not*.

I'm not talking about what we can or cannot know about the future. I'm talking about the *reality* that the future is not, in fact, *real*. It isn't *actual*. The notion that it exists is an illusion. The future is only, at most, *possible*.

There is but the present. There is *only* the present. There is only now, and now, and now, and. . . .

The only thing that's real—that's *really real*—is each now-moment. What is real is each "drop of experience," as process philosopher Alfred North Whitehead once put it. Indeed, what we call "time" can be best described as a "perpetual perishing."[1] This is why C. Robert Mesle, a philosopher who studies Whitehead, argues, "Time is like falling, I thought. We are always on the verge of falling forward into nothingness; but, in each moment, the world becomes anew, and the creative advance continues."[2] Each now-moment is the present unfolding of space-time. Time does not flow through space. Space does not flow through time. The two are entangled—at least if we take quantum mechanics seriously.

The present *is*. Actual. Real. Here. But it's not an object or a thing. It cannot be seized, regardless of what catchy Latin phrases might lead us to believe. Or, maybe it can, if we temper the language a bit: If it can't be "seized," the present—the in-process drop of experience we call "now"—*can* at least be *embraced*.

We can flow within its unfurling.

The future *is not*. Or, rather, is *not-yet*. The tantalizing potentialities that lure us in imagination and expectation are but an outgrowth of the present—always pregnant with possibility. But the future is not actual. It can't be.

∽

Why the Future Is a Problem

What is real is *now*: the now-moment that enfolds the past and unfolds into the next now-moment. The pulsing *now* of each instant is all that is. The rhythmic flows of "here" and "now" are the very substance of reality.

The future is not already out there, waiting to pop into existence. If that were the case now, then that's how it's always been—how it has always worked. And if that's how it has always worked, then you run into all kinds of theological problems: Terrible wars? Those were lying in wait. Genocide? That was part of the plan, apparently. Something bad happens to a loved one? Sorry! The author of space-time, call it God or whatever you'd like, wrote it into the story. Everything has to have a "greater purpose" in this paradigm. Even if the purpose is "inscrutable," the Author wrote it, so it must have been intended for some reason. If it happened, then it was part of some sort of already-existent future, just waiting for its time to shine. Everything's inevitable. Nothing's avoidable.

Yikes. I can hardly think of a worse theological position to take.

For this reason, whatever *is* is only ever the *here-now*. Whatever *is* is only ever the contraction of each present drop of experience, flowing into the next. But what is "next" is not predetermined, though it bears traces of the past. What is "next" is affected by the trajectory of the present: each moment influencing what follows. *Influencing*, not determining.

Thus, whatever hope is, it's not about the future. It's not for the future, of the future, nor in the future. Hope—if it's to be *really real*—is a phenomenon of the present.

☙

Radical Presence

If there's to be anything like care, compassion, or justice of any sort, it will only be possible because there was first a need that was *noticed*. All that is good is predicated on *noticing*, which is only possible by grounding ourselves in the here-now. By attuning ourselves to our environs—the critters, companions, and climate that make up our here-now—we open up the capacity to care for our common home.

Here's what I'm trying to get at in its most distilled form:

> *We cannot care for that which we've yet to notice.*
> *And we cannot notice without first slowing down.*

In the midst of a changing climate, attuning ourselves to the unending fluctuations we face daily could hardly be more important. The unfolding of each present moment enfolds the devastations of carbon emissions, toxic pollution, and ecological desecration. The pulsing of their effects has launched us into unknown territory and onto uncertain trajectories. Whatever we imagine the future to be *is not*. At least not—*yet*.

If there's such a thing as hope, it's not about what happens tomorrow or next year or next century. Yes, it bears the weight of all the possible trajectories that might obliterate life of all kinds, but only as they might incarnate in our present.

If hope is anything at all, it is, to draw on Black feminist critical theorist Tina Campt's language, "that which will have had to happen."[3] And this hope can only be possible if we first become grounded in the present, plunging our senses in the wholly here-and-now.

What might this mean for us—that is, the stilling of ourselves enough to practice deep listening to the present? Could this not be a way to better understand "prayer"—the attunement of our will to the needs of a world craving love and repair?

Hence, the chapters in this section are primarily about *prayerful attention* and what it means to cultivate it in a rapidly changing climate. The chapters that follow ask, How do we embody compassionate presence in an ever-quickening world? And (why) should we?

෨

Still Here

It's still cold outside, and I'm still looking out the same smudged window. The light is different, the shadows have shifted, and my cat is somewhere else.

I'm still, though, *here.* In a way, I always have been.

Sometimes, the present is something we notice our way into. Pause. Breathe. Take in. Attune—prayerfully.

Other times, it confronts us. Like now: I know where my cat is, because she has decided to bat a broken piece of window blinds across the kitchen floor. Such is life when you open your space to more-than-human kin.

I suppose it's worth noting, then, that what's at stake in all of this is not only "whether" we embrace the present but *how. How* are we to embrace the pulsing *now* from which we emerge, somehow, anew? How might this lead us *not* to solipsism—a self-obsessed myopia—but rather to an attunement to the relational webs that constitute us? In other words, how might the embrace of our *now* not shield us from our responsibilities to "those who come after" but, instead, lure us into more intimate connections that draw us outside of ourselves for the sake of hopeful justice?

My cat has returned to "her" window. She rests on the radiator, welcoming its warmth. And I am writing these words.

Still here. Always now.

Birding

A Question in the Garlic Field

Mud. So much mud. That's one of the things I remember most.

Sometimes—honestly, often—the timing for a harvest is hardly ideal. At least, it is when you're growing organically and working by hand. These days, the inconsistencies of day-to-day weather and the broader unpredictabilities of our fluctuating climate have made it increasingly difficult. Seasons shift suddenly, reversing without notice before skipping forward as though months had passed—all in the span of a few days. Ask any farmer, and they'll tell you: The climate is changing. There's no debate.

But what else is one to do when the garlic needs to be pulled and dried? Let it rot in the mud? Surely not.

So, we harvested, our backs bent in the haze of a misty morning—the condensation from recent rains hanging around as though it wanted to see the mess it had made of these garlic beds. Too wet to pull it out by the stalks, weakened by the moisture, our hands instead plunged into the mud to free the alliaceous bulbs. The work—though difficult—was joyful.

I hadn't planned to be a part of this harvest. I wasn't there when the garlic was planted, and I didn't even know I would be living in the Ohio River Valley when it was planted. Frankly, some nine months prior, I'm not sure I could have pointed out Cincinnati on a map without help, indistinguishable in my mind from the other

Cs—Columbus and Cleveland—that make up much of Ohio's population. I've learned quite a bit since.

I think we'd been in town for no more than three weeks, still unpacking and adjusting to a small apartment in an odd part of town. My job teaching theology wouldn't begin until the fall semester started in late August, so we tried to settle into our new community the way we knew best: food.

My partner found a magazine at a nearby farmer's market with information about local community-supported agriculture (CSA) farms. When we came across the description of an organic, regenerative, woman-owned farm—offering sliding-scale options to ensure that their produce was accessible to many—there was no question where wanted to get our veggies. We knew this was who we wanted to put our faith in. The name of the farm? No surprise: *Mustard Seed*.

We arrived at the first pickup of our farm-share thinking we'd depart with produce and maybe a recipe or two. But when you run into farmers distributing organic goods on the corner of a blue-collar neighborhood and you see tattoos of St. Francis of Assisi—and, wait, was that *kyrie eleison* in Greek on one of their wrists?—you have to ask questions. So when those farmers invite you to a communal garlic harvest the following day, after you've moved to a city where you know not a single soul, you accept enthusiastically, no matter how timid or introverted you may be feeling.

We made our way through the beds "inch by inch and row by row," as the folk song goes. Our boots sticking to the soil, we gathered the garlic, doing our best to keep the varieties separate, though the mud made that almost unmanageable. Working alongside the head farmer, Marykate, I noticed her stop what she was doing, stand upright, and look toward the trees lining the land. Then, she asked,

"Who is that?"

I hadn't seen or heard a thing. What did I miss? Her gaze traveled upward toward the treetops. None of this made any sense to me.

Maybe I shouldn't have accepted the invitation after all? I was out on a remote piece of land surrounded entirely by strangers, save my partner.

"Who is that?" she repeated.

Then I realized: Marykate heard a birdcall. She had heard a bird and asked, "Who is that?" Those three words wrecked me.

Indigenous botanist Robin Wall Kimmerer writes, "English doesn't give us many tools for incorporating respect for animacy. In English, you are either a human or a thing. Our grammar boxes us in by the choice of reducing a nonhuman being to an it."[1] By comparison, "In Potawatomi and most other indigenous languages, we use the same words to address the living world as we use for our family. Because they are our family."[2] There is power in our language.

As Kimmerer argues, when a "tree is not a who, but an it, we make that maple an object; we put a barrier between us, absolving ourselves of moral responsibility and opening the door to exploitation. Saying it makes a living land into 'natural resources.' If a maple is an it, we can take up the chain saw."[3] Marykate knew this well.

Who is that? *Who*. Not "what."

That bird is not a "what." Not a thing. Not an object. Religious scholar Thomas Berry was right: "With the rise of the modern sciences we began to think of the universe as a collection of objects rather than a communion of subjects."[4] And this wasn't some distant "we." It was me. I had absorbed this illusion, too.

And so it was that a single question in the middle of a muddy garlic bed made me rethink just about everything.

How different things might be if we simply asked, "Who is that?"

⌒

Confessions of a Birding Skeptic

Let me just get all of my confessions out of the way now so that you at least know that I'm being honest with you.

That moment in Marykate's garlic field is now but a memory from some years ago.

I'd be lying if I said that my interest in birds grew immediately and substantially, that this encounter was my ornithological conversion on the road to Emmaus (I'll spare you an emu pun). It wasn't: probably because I'm stubborn.

To be sure, the question made me rethink quite a lot. I'm not lying when I say that Marykate's question changed my worldview. I changed my language in an attempt to reframe my relationship to Earth. I sought to honor the animacy of the more-than-human world as best I could. And I tried to share these ideas with others—students, friends, family, though not strangers because that might be a little weird.

Did it make me care significantly about birds? Not really. Or not in any sort of monumentally different kind of way. To play with a bit of oxymoronic language, I suppose I had practiced a kind of compassionate indifference toward birds. I liked them, sure. They were around. I liked them being around, and I didn't want them not around, never mind struggling to flourish.

But were the birds themselves intrinsic to my understanding of the world or my own place in it? Far from it. Or, to add some foreshadowing, not *yet* anyway. That Marykate's question happened to be in reference to a bird was inconsequential. It could have been in reference to a toad or vole or cicada, and it still would have rocked me. The bird was merely the conduit for this perspective shift.

It wasn't until recently, now a handful of years removed from that muddy field, that I decided that I would actually *try* to care about birds. The idea of going "birding" still felt like some kind of joke. Having spent most of my life mountain biking, rock climbing, and surfing, "birding" just seemed kind of goofy. I mean, sometimes, I even find hiking to be boring—too slow. Now, I was basically going to don ambiguously tan-colored clothing and go hiking with some obnoxious-looking binoculars around my neck. Great.

But, in all seriousness, "birding" embodied just about everything

I had been seeking: an act of slowness that would encourage me to be curious, to learn, to listen. I figured it'd be good for my ecological knowledge as well as my mental health. Two birds with one . . . never mind. In any case, a lot of folks I admire—and quite like, for that matter—were fond of birding. So, how bad could it be?

I think it's too early to say that birds changed my life, but I feel pretty confident in making that claim. My avian revelation is recent, and I don't want to come across as hasty or insincere.

That revelation?

∽

Actually, Deeply Listening

Birding, bird-watching, whatever you want to call it, made me realize that I've never *actually, deeply* listened.

To be sure, I've listened closely: absorbing the crackles of a campfire, recognizing the tremble in a student's voice as they recount a recent hardship, noting the tin of a hi-hat or key-clacks of a saxophone, clocking a sharp inhale before a beloved shares something important.

But none of this is what composer Pauline Oliveros would describe as deep listening: "Listening in every possible way to every thing possible to hear no matter what you are doing."[5] This isn't just a matter of "hearing" but of *listening.* In Oliveros's words, "To hear is the physical means that enables perception. To listen is *to give attention* to what is perceived both acoustically and psychologically."[6] What's at stake in birding is not just "perception" but the *giving of one's whole attention to the perceived.*

In her book *How to Do Nothing,* artist and relatively recent bird-watching convert Jenny Odell quips, "I've always found it funny that it's called bird-watching, because half if not more of bird-watching is actually bird-listening. (I personally think they should just rename it 'bird-noticing.')"[7] Odell reasons, "You can't really look for birds; you can't make a bird come out and identify itself to you. The most you can do is walk quietly and wait until you hear something, and then stand motionless under a tree, using your animal senses to figure out where and what it is."[8] Or whom.

There's a certain way that birding well requires the faithful act of *doing nothing*, which isn't *actually* "nothing" as such. As Odell notes, "The 'nothing' that I propose is only nothing from the point of view of capitalist productivity."[9]

This is Odell's very point: the economies that prey on our attention—for example, social media platforms being intentionally designed to be addictive through features such as "infinite scroll"—keep us utterly inattentive to the beings who surround us and the bioregions we share with them. By capitalizing on our attention, we in fact pay these corporations *with our attention*. Anyone who's exited the wormhole of an hours-long digital binge knows that they couldn't have been any more *inattentive* than they were while swiping endlessly. Hence, this mindlessness is not at all what Odell means by "doing nothing." It's the opposite: "the ultimate goal of 'doing nothing' is to wrest our focus from the attention economy and replant it in the public, physical realm."[10]

Anthropologist Anna Tsing proposes that a world wrecked by capitalist technologies that have now gone so far as to quantify and profit simply from human attention needs renewed "arts of noticing."[11] In a society where even the amount of time we spend watching a single video in a string of countless others is measured, analyzed for its content, and then figured into future snippets to algorithmically place in our way, the need for stillness and mindfulness couldn't be greater. The machine of capitalism cannot tolerate unproductivity, hence it can find no intrinsic value in birds (save those that can be *made productive* as meat for humans, like chickens and turkeys). Noticing birds is, thus, not nothing at all: it is only "nothing" when viewed through the lens of capitalism.

I'd like to make the case, then, that this art of noticing might prove effective for exiting these attention economies, allowing us to reenter the multitudinous ecologies of each place in which we find ourselves.

How so? My experience of birding resembles Odell's, who writes,

> What amazed and humbled me about bird-watching was the way it changed the granularity of my perception, which had been pretty "low-res." At first, I just noticed birdsong more. Of course it had been there all along, but now that I was paying attention to it, I realized that it was almost everywhere, all day, all the time. And then, one by one, I started learning each song and associating it with a bird.[12]

Even after just a few days of wandering in the woods like the silly white retirees I'd smirked at in my past, I was completely overwhelmed. Birdsong "almost everywhere, all day, all the time." I didn't even notice—which is to say *perceive*—it before, never mind the characteristic calls and songs from varying species. Yeah, I knew what a crow and a mourning dove and a seagull sounded like before this. But the *wichity-wichity-wichity* calls of a common yellowthroat or the *peter-peter-peter* whistles of a tufted titmouse? Not a chance.

How might birding be a parable—inviting new lifeways amid the ruins of industrialism?

Birding requires a shift in our being: learning to silently listen—*wholly*—while also noticing flickers of light in a canopy or flashes of movement in the understory, all the while paying attention to *when* and *where* we are. Tuning into our timescape and landscape by means of our animal senses reminds us that we are not simply brains that carry around a body with them as an afterthought. We *belong* to Earth; Earth created us, too. Thus, birding is a practice that brings us into our bodies, noticing our own place in the great "communion of subjects," which becomes readily apparent when we begin to realize just how loud we often are (and, ironically, how little birds seem to like our boisterousness).

I wonder if this, too, is what Jesus might have been hinting at when he advised his audience to "consider the birds of the air."

⌇

On Care and Grief

Climate change demands critical care of our multispecies relationships and the ecologies that enmesh them, and none of this care is even possible without first *noticing* those who surround and suffuse us. Put simply, and to restate the guiding mantra of this section, we cannot care for that which we've yet to notice.

And there is a simultaneous grief and joy in this noticing: Grief that, since 1970, three billion birds in the United States—or nearly one in four birds—have been lost, indicating both critical collapses in our ecosystems and joy in the persistent pleasure that comes from encountering the few who remain. Environmental writer Terry Tempest Williams maintains the etymological and existential tension of "care," writing,

> "Care" is tied to the German root word *chara,* which means "to grieve" or "to lament." To care about wilderness is to grieve over what we have lost. To care about wilderness is to fall back in love with the world and lament how lost we are, and how lonely we have become.[13]

To notice and thus—maybe, ideally, hopefully—care about the many habitats and inhabitants of this planet suggests an opportunity to live out the vision of philosopher Alfred North Whitehead's definition of God: "a tender care that nothing be lost."[14] Of course, we ourselves cannot *ensure* that nothing is lost, and the overwhelming loss of species, cultures, languages, and lifeways—whether through colonialism, genocide, development, urbanization, or the like—illustrates the hellish injustices that have long plagued human communities, especially those in the industrialized West. Yet noticing remains that first crucial step for our witnessing to a divinely "tender care."

Without noticing "the birds of the air," we risk the continued collapse of not just our neighbors but, further, the ecosystemic webs that sustain life for us all. In so doing, we slide further into the loneliness bred by capitalism, which cannot create meaningful communities but only more and more and more capital. Thus, Odell's brilliant reminder: "To capitalist logic, which thrives on myopia and dissatisfaction, there may indeed be something dangerous about something as pedestrian as doing nothing: escaping laterally toward each other, we might just find that everything we wanted is already here."[15]

Birding unfolds possibility: deepened listening elicits careful noticing, which elicits bioregional wisdom, which elicits environmental justice, which elicits renewed deepened listening. . . .

By birding, we begin to hone our senses, learning to exit the death-drive of unfettered capitalism and instead *attend* to the many creatures and many locales they—which is to say *we*—call home.

∽

See Owl?

How do you describe the feeling of a goodbye party? "Bittersweet" doesn't quite cut it. It lacks the depth of feeling needed to convey the joys that a new season for a dear one will bring while also acknowledging the sorrows of knowing that that season will not be "*here*" or with "*us*."

So it was that the mix of nostalgia, eagerness, and lament braided through the bitter smoke of our makeshift backyard bonfire. Companions gathered around the potluck dishes that had been thrown together for the occasion, inevitably becoming one of those dinners that is predominantly snacks and sweets.

The late summer dusk settled in, everything but the fire a muted indigo.

I can't recall if it was a gasp or gesture or what exactly drew our attention to the branches just over our heads. But I know I looked, and so did everyone else.

A barred owl swooped onto a limb just above us. It sat stoically for only a moment—no longer—before continuing on to the trees ahead, just beyond our vision.

We were taken aback to have had this chance encounter in our neighborhood, feeling the kind of solemnity that only an owl can prompt. Stories wove their way through the backyard—of this owl, of others.

It wasn't long before one of the children alongside us, Damian, made it apparent he missed the sighting. He wasn't quite two years old at this point, but his imagination was already enraptured by birds.

Even before he was talking in a language properly understandable to others, Damian wouldn't let you miss a bird nearby. On walks with his father, he'd lean as far out of his stroller as possible to point and exclaim, "DEEDOW!" Robins on phone lines? "DEE-DOW!" Crows overhead? "DEEDOW!" No one knows where he got this "word" from, but we all knew what he meant.

Damian hadn't seen the owl, but he knew he had missed something. He understood clearly that the adults around him were moved in some way. And his curious mind wouldn't let it go.

For weeks, regardless of where he was, he'd ask, "See owl?" Or he'd recite, seemingly without end, "Owl flew away," which really sounded more like, "*ow foo way.*" He anticipated another owl, even if he was indoors or in some urban area.

For *weeks,* he wouldn't let it go. Just ask his parents, who, despite being some of the most patient people I know, began to tire of the refrain. On repeat: "Fire. Hot. See owl? Owl flew away. See owl? Fire . . ."

Some might say that he was stuck in the past, desperately trying to relive the moment and thus change his experience of it. Others might say that he was actually trying to see the very owl that briefly attended our gathering that eve.

I prefer to think that it was different.

For Damian, each moment was full of possibility. Each instant was charged with significance: the impossible was not actually so. He was fully expectant and thus fully present in each moment, embodying hope by noticing.

Sometimes, I like to think that he was, in his own way, reminding us of what Jewish philosopher Walter Benjamin had to say about time: "For every second was the small gateway in time through which the Messiah might enter."[16]

Every second opens to the infinite.

See owl.

∽

Birdsong

❧

There's little else as gratifying as learning the calls and songs of even just a few species. It's perhaps the best way to learn who surrounds you.

Start with the species that are most common in your area, including birds you might think of as "boring" or "mundane." Begin to familiarize yourself with those prevalent birds: for me, that's house sparrows, American robins, northern cardinals, mourning doves, and Carolina wrens. It'll differ for you depending on where you find yourself.

You can simply notice who makes which calls by observing them. Or you can seek help from astonishingly helpful—and often free—technologies. (One example that currently exists at the time of this book's publication is the Cornell Lab's Merlin Bird ID app.)

With repetition and reinforcement, these calls will become familiar to you. And there is some comfort in this familiarity, a warmth of knowing, "Ah, yes, there you are, Blue Jay—announcing your presence, celebrating your life."

Why comfort? Terry Tempest Williams could help us here: "Our experiences with the wild strengthen us and provide us with uncommon insights capable of moving toward an evolutionary grace that enables us to be in relationship with all beings."[17]

There's an evolutionary grace that emerges in not just *hearing* but in *listening to* birdsong. As we do, we might begin to not just hear but to *listen* to the "cry of the earth, cry of the poor."[18]

> *And maybe then we will know—*
> *faithfully and intimately—*
> *the answer to the question "Who is that?"*

Foraging

A Flame in the Forest

We stumble down the slick trail, damp from recent late-afternoon storms.

The roots crawling across our path glisten, beautiful but a siren call for those who wish to slip—or worse. We follow striped gneiss shelves and pass through fields dotted with boulders that shook loose from those same shelves who-knows-how-long ago.

The ferns that unfurl near the trail hold tiny orbs of water in their fingers, which means that my legs, at least from the knee down, are wet. But it's a typically humid day, so everything's wet.

But when you know, you know. So we continue to look.

Except we don't really "look." That's not quite the right word for it. When you look too hard for what you want, you miss what's actually in front of you. We sort of just . . . scan: not for what we want but for clues. Hints. Signs. We're "on the mystery."[1]

A recently downed tree across the ridge catches our eye. Thinking it was an oak from its ridged bark, we head toward it before realizing that it was yet another victim of the emerald ash borer. A massive red maple invites us to circle its base for traces but—none. We tread on.

We stumble upward without much confidence. But, like a small wildfire, it catches our eye. A beacon, aflame with an otherworldly orange: *Laetiporus sulphureus,* chicken of the woods.

On a soggy oak, decomposing on the hillside far above where we expected it, the tangerine hue of the mushroom beckons us.

We marvel at our fortune to find a cluster so large and so fresh, especially since that's not even what we were foraging for. A pocketknife is procured from a pack, and, knowing there are no poisonous lookalikes of this species, we carefully harvest the mushroom, ensuring it remains intact where it meets the bark so that it might continue to fruit in the future.

Our dinner plans have changed. Mushroom is on the menu. Knowing that this variety stores rather poorly, we'll have to find friends and neighbors to join us. A beautiful "problem" to solve.

We spend the evening cleaning our bounty. Slicing and cooking ensue.

The taste of love delights.

⌘

Practicing Foraging

Foraging refers to the practice of locating and harvesting foodstuffs "in the wild"—basically anywhere other than a farm or vendor. This might mean searching for edible mushrooms in a forest or gathering blackberries in a park or scavenging lambsquarters growing next to the sidewalk. It can happen in rural and urban spaces alike, though each presents its own unique challenges and opportunities.

Foraging requires an openness of the senses and an expansiveness of perception. To forage is to *notice*—to notice not just *what* but *when* and *where* and *how*.

Foraging is fundamentally a matter of "when": Is it the right season for that which you search? Has there been adequate rainfall? Too much rainfall? Is the time of day conducive for that thing (especially the case with flowers)?

Equally, foraging is a matter of "where": Are you in the right region? The right ecosystem or bioregion? Might it be advantageous to search more in the shade? The sun?

And often the "how" explains the relationship between the when and where: How does that plant grow? How does rain encourage mushroom fruiting? How might leaf pattern help distinguish this bramble from that?

Often, looking for "things in themselves"—whether fruits or grains or fungi—doesn't work. Scouring a place for the exact thing that one seeks is foolhardy. You might get lucky and stumble your way into something, as I have, but the search is far more successful when looking for contextual clues: leaf size, leaf hue, flower shape, height, distance to water source, companion species, amount of sunlight, undulation of terrain, and so forth. If birding is a practice of deep listening, foraging is the visual analogue.

≔

Foraging Honorably

What gives one the "right" to forage? Whose food is this to take? And once it's found, is one simply to take? And take? And take?

Foraging raises a number of concerns about land use, "ownership," history, and so forth. It opens queries about private versus public lands and all sorts of other qualms pertaining to who can be where—and why. Of course, this line of thinking is colonial through and through. Land ownership and land rights are relatively new ideas, stemming from the colonial project to subjugate and dominate territories and their inhabitants—at least on the land presently known as the United States.

There's an undergirding theological idea that lends itself to the atrocities carried out in both past and present settler-colonial practices in the Americas. In the first chapter of the Genesis creation song, we get this potent and patently abused verse: "God blessed them, and God said to them, 'Be fruitful and multiply and fill the earth and subdue it and *have dominion over* the fish of the sea and over the birds of the air and over every living thing that moves upon the earth'" (Gen. 1:28). This verse is often cited by some as the justification for all kinds of human behaviors: meat-eating, fishing, mining, logging, damming, and the like. Of course, the following verse makes it clear that the idyllic world of Genesis is, in fact, a vegan paradise:

> God said, "See, I have given you every plant yielding seed that is upon the face of all the earth and every tree with seed in its fruit; you shall have them for food. And to every beast of the earth and to every bird of the air and to everything that creeps on the earth, everything that has the breath of life, I have given every green plant for food." (Gen. 1:29–30)

Nothing but plants are to be eaten—whether by human animals or nonhuman animals. So even to interpret the prior verse about "dominion" as granting humans authority to "use" Earth as we please is hardly a faithful rendering. (Isn't it amazing that we can miss this stuff when the verses are *literally* back to back?) "Dominion" here doesn't even seem to imply meat-eating, let alone fracking, strip mining, or clear-cutting.

Nevertheless, the misinterpreted notion of "dominion" from the Genesis narrative gave rise to an anthropocentric—that is, human-centered—worldview of human supremacy, only to be amplified by the so-called doctrine of discovery that was advocated by Catholic popes, among others. Various Catholic decrees—including papal bulls by Pope Nicholas V in 1452 and 1455 as well as Pope Alexander VI in 1493—ordained the forced conversion and colonization of indigenous inhabitants of the Americas.[2] It is not accidental, then, that the colonizers—with all of the violence they wrought—were Christian, for the imperial theology of the Church sanctioned them "to bring under your sway the said mainlands and islands with their residents and inhabitants and to bring them to the Catholic faith."[3] This theology built on previous instructions in another context to

Invade, search out, capture and subjugate the Saracens and pagans and any other unbelievers and enemies of Christ wherever they may be, as well as their kingdoms, duchies, counties, principalities, and other property . . . and to reduce their persons into perpetual slavery.[4]

Colonization, slavery, and commodification of land: these are all *central* to the history of the institutionalized church.[5] Hence the import to "own" land is inseparable from colonialism and the theological impulse that drives it.

Dominion need not be synonymous with *domination*. Any conception of dominion that divorces it from responsibility is treacherous.

Without this history, even "rights" on their own is a bit of a conundrum. How interesting it is, for example, that a nation-state like the United States has a Bill of Rights but not a Bill of Responsibilities. The colonial mindset perceives "rights" as synonymous with "entitlements," even if they're framed as entitlements to be "free from" this or that.[6] But what are rights without responsibilities?

Responsibility implies reciprocity, and reciprocity suggests a *relationship*. If relationships suggest some sort of circularity, wherein each party contributes to and benefits from the other, then an entitlement mindset, which focuses only on rights and not responsibilities, is something of a unidirectional vector: a line that points one way and to one party's sole benefit. Rights are focused on "me"; responsibility is focused on "us." Rights are *incomplete* without responsibilities.

What might happen if we reframed our communities because we noticed the dynamic relationship between rights and responsibilities? What if we were to ask: To whom am I responsible, rather than, What right do I have? What if we interacted with our place and its many inhabitants out of a spirit of responsibility thereto and not a concern for what rights entitle me to be free from their accountability?

Before continuing any further, it must be said that many have had to fight for far too long for their rights—not least Black, femme, queer, and disabled folks in the US context. Furthermore, the wholesale erasure of indigenous autonomy by colonizers makes this country's founding on the supposed notion of liberty a hypocrisy, if not worse. The suggestion that "rights are incomplete without responsibilities" is not a condemnation of the liberative struggle for racial justice, gender justice, indigenous sovereignty, or the like. The liberative struggle for justice is not mutually exclusive from the responsibilities that complete the struggled-for rights. In fact, it is the *responsibility* of those who "have rights" to ensure that all members of their community *equitably enjoy* those same rights.

It's also not the case that rights cannot be used for liberative ends. Rights have long been used to safeguard land from exploitative businesses, protect water from polluting industries, and defend the autonomy of disenfranchised communities. Recent examples of this are manifest in the activism of water protectors at Standing Rock, of Wet'suwet'en blockades of the Coastal GasLink pipeline, and forest defense resistance to Atlanta's Cop City. In other words, insofar as our communities remain committed to the notion of rights, they cannot do so without a robust interest in the practice of responsibilities.

All of this is to say that the question about a forager's rights is incomplete without a discussion of their *responsibilities*. It is impossible to attend to whether one has a right to forage in the abstract—devoid of context, bioregion, season, history, inhabitants, and the like. That question can only be answered in light of the *relationship* one builds with a particular place and those who steward it. But the question of a forager's *responsibilities* persists.

Indigenous botanist Robin Wall Kimmerer offers a key paradigm for understanding a forager's responsibilities, which she terms the Honorable Harvest. She distills the Honorable Harvest into several key principles:

* Know the ways of the ones who take care of you, so that you may take care of them.
* Introduce yourself. Be accountable as the one who comes asking for life.
* Ask permission before taking. Abide by the answer.
* Never take the first. Never take the last.
* Take only what you need.
* Take only that which is given.
* Never take more than half. Leave some for others.
* Harvest in a way that minimizes harm.
* Use it respectfully. Never waste what you have taken.
* Share.
* Give thanks for what you have been given.
* Give a gift, in reciprocity for what you have taken.
* Sustain the ones who sustain you and the earth will last forever.[7]

Kimmerer is fundamentally concerned with what it means to be responsible, and she builds her ethic on the bedrock of responsibility. Notice the intentional relational reciprocity at the core of these teachings. One does not have an intrinsic "right" to simply take. Rather, one can only take if one is in right relationship to and *is thus responsible to* that place and its many beings. Even if one has received permission through deep listening and abiding, the harvest isn't the forager's alone: "Share," Kimmerer reminds.

Foraging ceases to be a practice of taking but instead becomes a cyclical relationship of responsibility in which the forager must be committed to flourishing. Kimmerer elaborates, "The teachings tell us that a harvest is made honorable by what you give in return for what you take. . . . A harvest is made honorable when it sustains the giver as well as the taker."[8] One's responsibility is always in relationship to one's place and the creatures who compose it. That is, what it means to be responsible is contingent upon where and when one is, which is not to say that responsibility is a posttruth, relativistic free-for-all and can mean whatever we want it to mean. Far from it. What this means is simply that the particularities of boreal forests differ from coastal wetlands, which differ from alpine meadows, which differ from temperate prairies, which differ from. . . . And, thus, to practice relational reciprocity in each context changes with each context. We must be *in touch* with our place.

Relationalism is not relativism.

☙

Foraging Relationally

Foraging is a risky practice—that is, when one lacks the proper knowledge to do so safely. The same is true for most any other facet of life: driving a car, operating a food processor, doing a cartwheel, and so forth. Lack adequate knowledge and you end up driving off a cliff or eating a fatal lookalike.

But foraging isn't *inherently* risky, per se. *Knowledge*, or lack thereof, dictates the risk. Yet the kind of knowledge needed to forage both safely and responsibly is not strictly a "technical" knowledge. There certainly is technical knowledge required to forage safely: identification of leaf shape, stem characteristics, flower size, fruit color, and so many other matters. This technical knowledge, however, is only and thoroughly *relational*.

First, one must develop a personal relationship to their place, which is always changing, always becoming. One must develop a relationship to weather and seasons, minding patterns, precipitation, and other particularities. How does a plant in this particular place change in shape, size, and color throughout its life cycle? How does this region respond to rainfall? What critters are passing through the area in each season? The peculiarities of each bioregion differ from the next. Developing a relation to land is paramount.

And since traditional tools like the *Farmer's Almanac* or USDA Plant Hardiness zones are limited at best, and are becoming increasingly less reliable as our climate shifts nonlinearly, other sources of wisdom are needed.

Thus, second, one must develop a relationship with the persons who already have relationships developed with that place. The know-how of foraging is complex: knowing when and where to forage, which species to harvest, how to navigate the terrain, how not to overharvest, and so on all require a *wisdom* cultivated through years of practice. Indeed, the practice of foraging cultivates something far more akin to *wisdom* than to knowledge. Field guides and online sources can be very helpful, but they're also insufficient. There's only so much you can learn from an anatomical drawing of a plant. Becoming acquainted with that plant, introducing yourself to it, observing it, and thus displaying gratitude to it are needed to fulfill the call to harvest honorably, and this is often best done with a human guide who already practices in this way. The wisdom of those who belong to the land they tread—which is to say, often, indigenous persons—prevails and routinely surpasses any other.

Rabbi Abraham Joshua Heschel contends, "Knowledge is fostered by curiosity. Wisdom is fostered by awe."[9] Foraging well— which is to say honorably and relationally—occurs only through experiencing awe *for* and *among* our creaturely world: the miracle of morels, the pungency of ramps, the delight of pawpaws. To be enraptured by the goodness of our environs stimulates an awesome love. To this end, Kimmerer reminds, "One of our responsibilities as human people is to find ways to enter into reciprocity with the more-than-human world. We can do it through gratitude, through ceremony, through land stewardship, science, art, and in everyday acts of practical reverence."[10]

Careful noticing is the means by which we enter into relationship with that which grounds our being. Let us not *pay* so much as *gift* our attention.

cℐ

Berry Hunting

We wandered more than foraged, really. Trekked down hills, scoured forest-side. We roamed in the summer heat.

There was rumored to be a large patch of black raspberries here. Or so we'd been told. Hence, with dear friends and their newborn—strapped to Mom's chest—we hunted for the brambles that might gift us the confluence of sour-sweet that no artificial flavor could approach.

"Near the bend in the path not far from the pond," they said. Helpful, except that there were many bends and several ponds.

We noted muscadine grapevines, small sumac trees, and promising logs for mushrooms along the way. None bore fruit, but we squirreled the information away for the proper season.

We kept to the edges, where thorny briers shot out of the woods, but my eyes were drawn to the expanses between. I knew we'd not find anything to eat there, but that wasn't the source of my attraction. I marveled at what was, because it was so far from what had been.

The land we tread was once a golf course—and not long ago, either. The town reclaimed the space from the defunct country club: no longer exclusive to the wealthy elite who carted around manicured lawns that needed ungodly amounts of irrigation, the land became a commons once again.

Dandelion reemerged on hillsides. Plantain shot through the fairways. And milkweed returned, with the help of human companions.

It's far from perfect now—fossil-fuel-powered mowers still clear areas for "recreation" despite the endless sports complexes just down the road. The autonomy of the Miami, Shawnee, and Osage Peoples has not yet been acknowledged, nor their stewardship of this land since time immemorial. Noticing *what could yet be* is the grounds for hope-making. *What could yet become* allures.

Oh, and the black raspberries?

We found them. But we were too late. We found only remnants. The mild winter and desperately hot spring ripened the fruit far earlier than we had anticipated. I guess this is the norm now in a climate-changed world—that is, if the brambles don't simply wither.

But we found a handful nevertheless, split them between ourselves, and made a pact to return next year.

We were grateful—for new life, for reclamation, for reemergence. For this land and its persistence, we give thanks, noticing new possibilities for reciprocal relation—in so doing, beginning to make hope amid disturbed landscapes.

Indeed, this hope is for nothing short of resurrection.

∽

Foraging Ramps

Where I live, ramps—a sweet-spicy allium sometimes referred to as "wild leeks"—are a delicacy. Their rich taste and ample adaptability make them a delight to cook with. But demand from bourgeois restaurateurs propped up by the digital attention economy have contributed to the gross overharvesting of this precious bulb. Ramp colonies that were once flourishing now dwindle—or worse.

Ramp seeds take as long as eighteen months to germinate. And ramps can take more than seven years to reproduce to full maturity. The detriment of overconsumption thus lasts decades.

Ramps are the entanglement of grief and joy. In a climate-changed world, anguish and delight are interwoven.

There are, however, ways to relish ramps *without* contributing to their destruction. By taking only one leaf from one plant (leaving the other to grow) and refraining from uprooting bulbs, ramps colonies can continue to multiply. Use a sharp knife to carefully remove a leaf. Be sure to harvest across the patch and not just in one concentrated area. Disperse disturbance, in other words.

As you take, practice gratitude. Ramps are one of the best plant partners with which to practice Kimmerer's "honorable harvest" in hopes that by "sustain[ing] the ones who sustain you the earth will last forever."

Or so I pray.

Composting

Dirt

You're dirt.

I don't mean that in any pejorative sort of way. I'm dirt, too. We are dirt.

It's kind of strange that "dirt" is kind of a "dirty" word. It doesn't have the best of connotations. I find this odd, since it's the very thing that keeps us alive.

You and I would not exist but for a layer of topsoil that is about six inches deep. Without it? Nothing. Well, nothing "human" anyway.

We tend to despise—or at the very least steer clear from—the very source of our life. We stray from our earthy maker.

Maybe you were once taught that getting dirty is bad. It is good to be clean: "Cleanliness is close to godliness" and other common lies. Maybe you still believe that to be clean is to be less earthly, less fleshly, and thus more heavenly. Dirtiness, impurity, and sinfulness all go hand in hand, it seems. That's the logic of it anyway.

In the West, we tend to think in hierarchies. Move up the so-called Great Chain of Being and things get less embodied, more spiritual. God's up there at the tippy-top—all spirit, no body. Pure. As you descend, things get more embodied and less spiritual. Angels. Humans (with "souls!"). Mammals. Birds. Fish. Insects (*definitely* no souls!). Plants. Minerals. Dirt.

Dirt: fleshy, inert, spiritless. The most earthen, the least divine.

This is what some expressions of Christianity would have us believe. And, from this thinking, you get all kinds of neat catch-phrases: "This world is not my home." "My real home is in heaven with Jesus." "I'm but a stranger here." So it goes.

If you couldn't already tell, I can hardly stand any of this. I'm not a fan—in part because this kind of thinking leads to an ethic of disdain toward Earth and its multiplex inhabitants. It creates superiority complexes that justify abuse—whether of mountains deemed lifeless and thus perfect for strip-mining, forests considered inanimate and thus worthy of clear-cutting, or humans deemed more animal-like and thus fit for enslaving. I'm not interested in theologies and ethics that give credence to violence.

This kind of hierarchical thinking is the theological "justification" for all kinds of sinful atrocities. Insofar as we disparage the terrestrial, we condemn the Earth to perpetual subjugation and commodification, indeed to *damnation.* So long as we maintain that the spirit and flesh—indeed the heavenly and earthly—are divorced, we will never find ways of making hope amid climate catastrophe. It just won't happen.

I also can't stand this hierarchical ideology because it has hardly any biblical precedent—at least not in the creation stories of the Hebrew Bible.

The second Genesis creation narrative (Gen. 2–3) challenges any sort of hierarchical thinking that presupposes a divorce of humans from Earth: "Then the Lord God formed the human (*adam*) from the dust of the ground (*adamah*) and breathed into his nostrils the breath of life." The *adam*—or "human" in Hebrew, which is just a regular ol' noun and not this human's "name," you should know!—is formed from *adamah*—or "topsoil." The Lord God forms the human from the soil.[1]

And since *adam* and *adamah* are etymologically related, it would make more sense to translate *adam* not as "human" so much as "Earthling." We could thus render it, "Then the Lord God formed the Earthling from the Earthground." Hence, our lives are "from dust to dust."

The English language also reflects this same intimacy. "Human" and "humus"—or the rich form of soil, organic matter, that enables life—are linguistically intertwined. The two are cut from the same . . . mud?

In the beginning, we were dirt. Since the beginning, we have always been dirt. The dirt of Genesis suggests nothing negative at all. And that would make sense, since *dirt is the genesis of all.*

You're dirt. I could hardly call you a more holy thing.

ℭℐ

The Nature of Nature

Compost is dirt. Or, as it happens, it's one of the many forms that "dirt" can take. More specifically, compost is the combination of green (or "wet") organic matter, such as food scraps, with brown (or "dry") organic matter, such as hay, that has broken down over time and with heat to form a dark substance often rich with nutrients that resembles soil. Composting, when done well, is an aerobic process, meaning it requires air to facilitate the breakdown of the organic matter by means of microbial activity. What was once a heap of distinguishable "things"—egg shells, lawn trimmings, springtails, coffee grounds, autumn leaves, apple cores, worms, twigs, bacteria—becomes something *entirely other.*

The simplest way to think about it would be:

$$organic\ matter + air + microorganisms$$
$$+ heat\ energy + time = compost$$

Framing it this way oversimplifies the act of composting, to be sure. Too wet, and your mixture won't break down. Not enough air, and it'll get *really* smelly. Too cool, and it'll take *forever* (or what feels like forever) to decompose. An imbalance of basic materials, and it may become too acidic. That there are few elements to it need not imply that it's simple, per se. Admittedly, I struggle with my own compost bin.

But also, this silly equation oversimplifies things because compost isn't really a linear process at all. It's more of a multiplicative sort of thing. The effects of altering just one element ripple with consequences in nonlinear ways. Heat and microorganismic activity drive the process, expanding and contracting time in their transformative potency. The change that occurs with compost is an entirely different sort of change than the ones we're often used to discussing. All of this, really, hinges on our concept of change. Paying attention to compost can reframe our perspective.

It's easy to think of the word "change" as denoting a simple linear progress of some sort. Change is often understood as *quantitative* change—that change is merely a matter of quantity or amount: think incremental reform, steady growth, smooth improvement. This idea about change leads us to think that there is some sort of *essence* at the base of all things, a *core* lying beneath the attributes that define it, some *kernel* "beneath" a thing's qualities that remains unaltered. If you've ever had the distinct joy of reading French philosopher René Descartes, you'll know that this sort of thinking is precisely what he proposed.

Let's use the example Descartes gives us to illustrate this point: candle wax.[2] Candle wax is weird because sometimes it's hot and liquidy, and other times it's cool and firm. It's true to say both of candle wax even though they are effectively opposite statements that describe incompatible states. Yet logically we know that wax cannot be both hot and cold at the same time, nor can it be solid and liquid at once. To resolve this tension, Descartes would argue that the wax exists independently of its attributes; there is an underlying waxness—an essence to wax—that endures somehow beneath the changes that occur to it. Regardless of whether it's hot, clear, and liquid or cool, opaque, and solid, it is still "wax" because it is, in its essence, an exemplification of waxness. Put simply, the core of any changing thing persists—somehow unchanged.

You might be on board with Descartes, thinking, *Yeah. Wax is wax. What else would it be?* But how can something exist independent of the attributes that define it? What is wax if not the characteristics that it simply *is*? Let's take it one step further.

This way of perceiving the world is similar to what's at stake in the famous Ship of Theseus puzzle. If a ship, over the course of many years of repair, eventually has all of its parts replaced, is it still the same ship? If, say, centuries down the line, none of the remaining parts are "original," as each was replaced one by one over those years, is it not the same ship? Is there some sort of essence—call it "shipness"—that exists independent of its parts, making it the same ship still?

And, if it's not the same ship, then there has to be a moment at which it became a *different* ship. At what precise point did it cease to be the same ship? When just one part was replaced? When it reached 51 percent replaced parts? One hundred percent replaced parts? *Why?*

Now consider compost.

How would this work with something like compost? At what point does so-called compost begin and end? When precisely does it *become* compost? When is it finally compost? Is it ever finally compost if it is always, perpetually changing—indeed decomposing?

What exactly is the essence of compost?

Let's make it even more complicated. Can something that is *decomposing* constantly have an essence that *composes* it? What is the underlying compostness at the heart of compost? If there is such a thing, wouldn't this mean that every component that can be added to a compost heap—like rinds or stalks or isopods or soldier flies—also possesses this essence of compost? If so, where is it? In its DNA? What about the components like carbon or oxygen that don't have DNA? When does this essence appear, or is it always there? Are you overwhelmed yet with all these questions?

I personally wouldn't know how to answer any of these questions (save the last one), because I don't find this way of thinking to be compelling or helpful or even accurate.

If we are to make sense of something like compost, we need a different paradigm.

Consider an alternative: What if we were to stop thinking about the world as a series of objects and things with essences but instead as a web of processes and becomings? I'm very tempted to get all philosophical (as my students might put it) right now, but let's just keep things simple and grounded.

Everything is always changing.

I look out my window and notice the weathering wood, chipping and cracking, on my creaky porch. The catalpa tree across the street offers shade with its immense leaves now, but those will yellow and fall off in some time. I inhale, noticing the air expand my chest. The wind outside invisibly moves the shrubs I can see from my desk, a small sign of large atmospheric events constantly in the process of moving, shifting, amplifying, diminishing. The breakfast I ate not long ago digests in my stomach as I resist the urge to scratch a bug bite that I got while gardening yesterday. Water ebbs and flows through my cell walls by means of osmosis—tidal.

I am porous. I am becoming. I am constantly changing.

Everything is always changing.

I live because of the ever-changing nature of the universe: the respiration I enjoy comes by virtue of the exchange of oxygen and carbon dioxide, the gift of carbon yielding organic life, among other things. Orbits, tides, jet streams, migrations, erosion: all is motion.

Nothing is static, bounded, self-reliant. All is interconnected, enmeshed, entangled. "No man [*sic*] is an island." No thing is an island.

Motion, change, flux is the very nature of nature. Without endless becoming, nothing would—*be*. What we think of as constant or fixed is really just a snapshot of change, a freezing of space-time that only ever *flows*.

The famed Greek philosopher Heraclitus seemed to know this

quite some time ago: you never step in the same river twice. And this is true not only because rivers are constantly changing, but so, too, are you! As am I. We step in the river anew each time. As Lauren Olamina, the protagonist of Octavia Butler's novel *The Parable of the Sower,* writes, "All that you touch You Change. All that you Change Changes you. The only lasting truth Is Change."[3] (She then goes on to suggest that, "God is Change," but I'll hold off on discussing that for another time.)

That all of reality is flux, I think, is part of the point of rituals. By performing the "same" thing routinely—whether frequenting a coffee shop or participating in the Eucharist, weekly dinners with beloveds or an exercise regimen—we observe the newness with which we engage in that "same" activity by virtue of the ways that we've *become.* We approach "sameness" with novelty, observing how we've been moved, shaped, formed since our last encounter with that ritual.

Back to compost.

I ask again: Where does compost begin and end? When is it first or when is it finally compost? Yes, there is a time, I suppose, when the soily substance that we're looking at meets the *definitional* qualities of what we've deemed compost. But we must remember that even that particular soily substance isn't still, static, stationary; it's always and only ever transforming, transmuting, transfiguring. What we call "compost" is simply a snapshot of the constant process of cycling nutrients, fluctuating energy, and chemical reactivities. It is only ever *ongoing.*

The very idea of "essences" decomposes in the compost heap.

And? So what?

Compost enables us to think of change altogether differently. It discloses that change can be *qualitative,* which is to say *transformative.* That onion skins and pill bugs and bark and air and heat become something *wholly other* is a radical exemplification of *creativity.* No version of *quantitative* change could ever capture the revolution that occurs in the heap. Compost empowers us to think in nonlinear terms by tuning into the potentialities of our place and the matters that compose it. There's hardly a more imagination-inspiring thing than dirt.

Think about the possibilities that might reveal themselves to us should we notice what compost teaches us. Compost might inspire us to break open our imaginations and break outside of the paradigms afforded to us. As a note for what's ahead, the remainder of this book will practice this sort of imagination.

∽

Transformation | Transfiguration

Nothing about compost reflects what came before it. The remnants of what "was" disappear, but their gifts are not forgotten or erased so much as transformed into new life and possibility. Compost deals in *conversion* of the most radical sort.

The process of composting makes our food supply chain into a circle as opposed to a unidirectional line. The cycling of nutrients at the "end" of this cycle enriches plants for further growth and a new *beginning*, rather than scraps ending in a landfill, benefiting no crop and producing considerable amounts of methane, thereby contributing to the greenhouse effects that are driving climate change.

With compost: no ends, no beginnings. Death has not the final word.

What if we were to reframe our spiritual lives through the lessons illustrated by compost? What might we *notice* and, thus, *bear witness to*? Might our own processes of conversion benefit from circularity—a return to the *ground of our being* in each instant?

The radical nature of compost's conversion is not a once-and-for-all thing. Its transformations are ongoing: possibility emerging from each instant, so long as one pays attention to the heap and its needs. To seek conversion in this vein, then, would not be a once-

and-for-all event but could only ever be a moment-by-moment decision, an embrace of the present and a transformation of death into life in each instant. It could only ever occur now, and now, and now, and. . . .

We, like compost, are not essences with changing characteristics. We are always processes of becoming; we are the conglomeration of each moment enriching the next, emerging anew each instant. Constantly becoming, endlessly transforming. The cyclical invitation to practice faithfulness—the pursuit of loving creativity—materializes in every now.

It would seem that to live a life inspired by compost would be to commit oneself to the *wholly other*, the *unimaginable*, indeed the *impossible*. We ourselves would decompose to the appetites of a self-obsessed society in which the status quo is marked by ruinous violence, instead bearing witness to the unthinkable. And what could be more other, more unimaginable, more impossible than the mysterious self-giving love that threads through the wisdoms of so many spiritual practices and religious traditions?

Through compost, we learn that some of the parables we live may be beyond repair. That is, by thinking with compost, we realize that some narratives may need to die in order that we might be resurrected into new life.

This extends beyond the "personal," too. In a world of political linearity, wherein social change and goodness, we are told, can only come from incrementally reforming the systems and structures that operate in and control much of our experience, to be converted by compost necessitates a wholesale rejection of those narratives in favor of parables of revolutionary love. And this isn't strictly spiritual either: the *qualitative* change incarnated by compost illuminates the kinds of shifts in our thinking that we likely need to survive climate change. If there is no reform (quantitative change) of capitalism, then we must revolutionize (qualitative change) our economies such that they align intimately with our ecologies.

Capitalism will never breed love—how could it? Racism, sexism, and homophobia are the opposite of compassion and thus cannot provoke it. Nationalism is a rejection of the beloved nature of the so-called Other. These insidious ideologies and the institutions they construct must be buried—indeed decomposed—for the possibility of hopeful resurrection.

By contemplating compost, we begin to see the need for our *transfiguration*: witnessing to the world imagined otherwise through revolutionary love. Notice, then, that this conversion is not an escapist heavenly fantasy so much as a *grounded* compassion—always and only ever here-and-now. "On earth as it is in heaven . . ."

For those of the Christian persuasion, I think this is what that confounding man from Nazareth meant by the kingdom of God: a beloved community in which there are no "firsts" or "lasts," a revolutionary people where neither inequity nor hierarchy can take root. Convince me of how capitalism—which only ever seeks to maximize profits at any cost—will usher in the kingdom of God, and I will eat my shoe. Making Earth heavenly will come not by capitalistic proclivities so much as through a composted imagination.

What exactly might a composted imagination yield?

First, compost asks us to consider what it means to create the conditions for transformation. We need not concern ourselves with change-making when it comes to compost; rather, compost asks us to attend to *the grounds for change*. What might we glean from staying present to *that which enables conversion*?

Compost also teaches us to notice processes of becoming and bear witness to them. What must we tune into to be transformed anew each and every instant?

Compost invites us to envisage possibilities that our present moment enables, asking: What are the conditions that *enliven*? That *multiply possibility*? What must we die to so that we might live transfigured lives?

If compost offers anything when it comes to redefining hope in the face of climate catastrophe, it's that hope is a process of creating the conditions for fecundity, but hope cannot create fecundity itself. A composted hope is, thus, not about achievement or finality or closure; it's, instead, committed to noticing what our ecologies offer as fodder for transfiguration. Weaving hope into the fabrics of our contexts would entail a boldness of imagination that would not allow our satisfaction with the misleading narratives of our present status quo; instead, it would catalyze our collaboration with the matters, resources, and companions in our communities in service of transfigured lifeways.

It would mean nothing short of inciting the resurrective capacities of our soils and, thus, our souls.

From the dust, we might be born again.

∽

Ritualizing Compost

❧

One of my chores in my household is taking out the food scraps from our kitchen, stowed in a little metal bin, to our compost tumbler out back.

For the record, I love compost. It takes a weird obsession with the stuff to write a book chapter about it. But, admittedly, I loathe "taking out the compost." It has nothing to do with compost itself. It's just my troubled relationship with household chores. I'm working on it.

For this reason, I've crafted this ritual for myself, but perhaps it will serve you, too. What does this practice seek? A grounding in, by, and through this becoming-ground.

❧

As you leave your home and approach the compost heap, notice how you're moving and what you're carrying with you:

> *Do you move with haste and thus irreverence?*
> *Or do you walk with intention, embracing each*
> *step as a gift? How do your movements reflect your*
> *interior life in this moment?*

Lift the lid off the bin.

> *What do you notice? Do the insects, oozes, and*
> *smells move you in some way? Why do you react as*

you do? Might you be reinforcing your socializa-
tion into a culture that despises the very things
that create life?

Pour the scraps into the heap, adding to them dry, brown organic matter.

Why do you compost? Do you practice this to rid
yourself of the guilt you feel for your many other
unsustainable actions? Is this your attempt to
atone for your environmental sins? Or do you do
so out of reverence? Out of faith in the possibility
of transfiguration? What is the prayer of this com-
post—for itself, for you?

Mix in the new materials to the heap.

Do you believe in the power of resurrection?
That life can come from death? What exactly do
you worship? How will you move in the wake of
this encounter?

Gathering

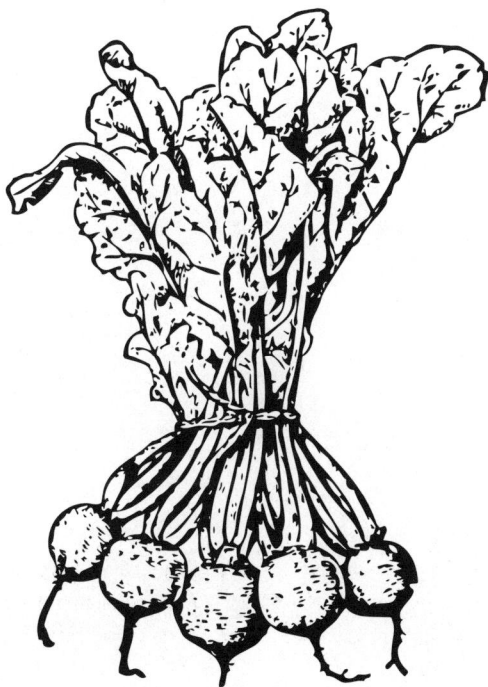

Surging Assembly

You look to the sky: a massive wave overhead.

Flickering dots whip through the air like a net blown about during a windstorm. The web thrashes without an anticipatable trajectory, yet its movements keep time more faithfully than a sophisticated orchestra.

There is no discernible order, though "chaotic" would be an antonymous descriptor for this roiling network, pulsing in all directions yet somehow and someway in sync—indeed *together*.

Waves. One after the next.

You catch glimpses of individuals, their wings beating the invisible air in this great dance. But the whole overwhelms the senses: Too much to take in, the countless Ones dart amid this ensemble of Many. There is no conductor, no puppet-master, directing Each in their assembly as All.

Ebbs. Flows. Planes. Waves. Endless waves. In a word? Murmuration.

A murmuration is an ornithological term to describe the collective flight patterns of starlings—the spheres and folds and loops that these birds perform. The name comes from the murmuring sound that the collective flapping of wings creates. Maybe you've seen one: the sky darkened by an amorphous avian cloud—flowing.

In a murmuration, there's no single leader and no pure followers. It is a self-organizing and improvisational kind of thing. No foreordained plan. No predestined conclusion. Just sheer and utter presence—in community.

Murmurations enfold and unfold, expanding and contracting without predetermination, instead adapting to their present and the beings amid it.

What can be learned from these clouds of birds? What of their *gathering*?

☙

Presence Is Communal

We will only be able to make hope in a climate-changed world by first grounding oneself in one's here-now, embodying the lessons taught by arts of noticing, like those of the previous chapters.

But it would be a mistake to think that practices of noticing are in service of hermitlike solipsism. Noticing draws us into an experience of presence but not one that would be individualistic in any sense. Reattuning our senses to the here-now reveals how caught up we are in our communities of climates, creatures, contexts, and cultures.

To be present is to be mindful of the utterly entangled nature of life itself. We *are* because of air and soil and water and plants and each other. Presence is the experience of interconnectedness as such. I exist in this moment, this place, this atmosphere, this climate. I am not only *because of* these things, but, in many ways, *I am* these things.

I had a poetry professor, Robert Carnevale, once say to my class, "We don't look each other in the eyes very often, because, when we do, we realize our indebtedness to one another." The presence that we embody in the simple but profound act of sharing eye contact yields the revelation that we exist by virtue of community. We can't begin to count how much we owe to each other, to Earth. It's something that no accounting—neither credit nor debt—could ever *actually* account for.

Yet, in a way, some of us owe more than others. As geographical theorist Kathryn Yusoff argues, global climate change "might seem to offer a dystopic future that laments the end of the world, but imperialism and ongoing (settler) colonialisms have been ending worlds for as long as they have been in existence."[1] The privileges of some come precisely at the expense of others. The violent histories of colonialism, racism, misogyny, and the like remind us that "the end of this world has already happened for some subjects."[2] Hence, Yusoff's claim:

> If the imagination of planetary peril coerces an ideal of "we," it only does so when the entrappings of late liberalism become threatened. This "we" negates all responsibility for how the wealth . . . was built off the subtending strata of indigenous genocide and erasure, slavery and carceral labor, and evades what that accumulation of wealth still makes possible in the present.[3]

The forces that have displaced peoples and dismantled geologies still remain in effect. And the temptation is to individualize our responses thereto. This temptation is why companies like BP have so ingeniously shifted the blame onto you and me by creating "tools" like the carbon footprint calculator: blame is deflected from multinational corporations that are ravaging Earth for the sake of short-term profit to individuals who are trapped in the rigged economies and are just trying to survive.[4]

Always, to be present is to be in relation to all of this. To be present is to be *in community*—ecological, economic, social, historical, and beyond. It's even true to say that we, as individuals, *are communities in and of ourselves.* We host countless microorganisms in our bodies, and these microorganisms, such as those of our gut microbiomes, enable our very existence as supposed individuals. When we cultivate habits of noticing, then, we do not necessarily unveil the experience of "the self" but, rather, of "the self-in-relation."

We are the confluence of matters, minerals, moments.

Thus, to be here and now is to exist at the nexus of possibility that is offered by unfolding—indeed unending—relations, grounded in that which is afforded by our ecological location, social location, resources, and beyond.

To be present means to be *gathered* into community. Precisely what kinds of communities we might seek to gather amid a changing climate is the subject of this section of the book.

Any such gathering can occur only through escape: exiting from the rugged individualism and egocentric tendencies of Western culture. If we understand the arts of noticing proposed earlier as a retreat from the narratives that suffuse us—for example, how capitalism teaches us that we are valuable only insofar as we are productive or how colonial Christianity teaches us that we are to dominate the Earth because of a mandate to have so-called do-minion—then we must come to recognize that this "exit" is also simultaneously a reentry: a reentry *into community.*

Artist Jenny Odell argues just this in her contention that seeking presence by practicing various arts of noticing is not actually about doing "nothing" at all. Rather, it's a triple-movement: "1) a drop-ping out . . . ; 2) a lateral movement outward to things and people that are around us; and 3) a movement downward into place."[5]

We exit in order to reenter—reconnected by bonds and bio-region.

Narratives of human exceptionalism or white supremacy or heterosexism are ones of dis-relation: they inhibit relationship for the sake of exploitation. These ideologies only "work" because they sever relational ties, thus rendering the world into static objects that are able to be commodified. Hence the ways in which the unending *distractions* of digital media and technologies keep us from more intimate and authentic relations: they keep us from being present to one another and the relationships that compose our world.

The distraction of a single starling could wreak havoc on a mur-muration, impeding the relational presence that is required to fly in formation as they do. Distractions inhibit intentional gathering.

The fundamental question here is this: As we become present, how might we reenter the world? Or, put differently, what parables might allow the gathering of collectives dedicated to prayerfully making hope in this ravaged world?

൦ᴣ

Seeing Each Other

My students huddle together in rickety chairs in a hay-strewn barn. They're cold but happy, giggling over hot drinks and swapping stories from the frigid creek. Silliness doesn't come too naturally for many of them. Their time in the US education system has beaten most of that out of them, along with their imagination and, sometimes, joy.

But a cold plunge changes things. So does a meal made with ingredients that they themselves harvested only hours earlier.

I try to create this sort of environment in our usual classroom. I really do try. But overcoming my students' assumption that education is strictly "intellectual" and not *incarnate,* of which they've been convinced after over a decade of formal schooling, is almost insurmountable. I have countless metaphors, activities, and witty quips to help them consider the possibility that they have a great deal to learn from each other and to learn from Earth—rather than just their turtleneck-wearing professor. When none of this works, my co-instructor and I gather with them on a homestead in a remote Appalachian river valley—to be near each other and near Earth.

Someone makes a joke about who will empty the composting toilet next, hoping their humor will shield them from confronting their own waste. Playing cards are shuffled, and the muffled stories around the bonfire outside the barn rise with the ashy smoke.

You'd think they'd known each other for years. For some, it's the most time they've spent with anyone besides their family since coming to college. Despite a year or two or three in the dorms already, they're just now beginning to see the goodness of communal life. It's not their fault that they hadn't before: no one had shown them.

One of the quieter ones stumbles in from the dark, headlamp askew and wearing countless layers: "Have you SEEN the *stars*!?"

Several dart out. Some of them have never actually, truly seen stars until this weekend.

Awe abounds.

This is the kind of education I've longed to practice—purposeful, particular, placed. This kind of education relies on recognizing our inability to learn in isolation, in a vacuum. We must first *gather*—in place, in community. Only then can education be seen not as a capitalist factory for the production of good (which is to say docile and unquestioning) workers but instead as an opportunity to practice critical compassion toward our world and its inhabitants. As Robin Wall Kimmerer asks, "Isn't this the purpose of education, to learn the nature of your own gifts and how to use them for good in the world?"[6] Learning thus becomes more than the consumption of knowledge, instead functioning as a means of embodying *responsibility*.

Late into the night, they'll continue to gather: in story, in song, in silence. Out here, they realize that they need each other, need Earth. Out here, they realize that it is good to be good. Away from the distracted cultures they swim in, they are learning to see in renewed ways.

In this gathering, my students are finally *seeing each other again for the first time*.

Seed-Saving

Judy's Kale

Do you like kale? No, I mean, do you *actually* like it? As in, *like* like it? No one else is listening. I promise I won't tell anyone if you say no. Frankly, I wouldn't blame you. It can be our secret.

Here's my story about kale.

Once upon a time, I decided that, if I was to go to graduate school to study theology, the only way I could justify it would be if I farmed full-time, too. I had never worked on a farm. I hadn't even gardened much, really. But I knew I needed to.

I had been studying biblical texts for a few years as an undergraduate, but despite being steeped in the texts' worlds and anguishing in the process of learning Biblical Hebrew, Greek, and Aramaic, I still felt detached.

I realized that I felt disconnected from the texts because they came from a thoroughly *agrarian* world and worldview. I came from suburbia, and my worldview was modern or postmodern or post-postmodern or something like that. Regardless, I didn't live my life by the seasons, in part due to the digital world that was suffusing my upbringing but also because I was raised in Southern California, where the two seasons are seventy degrees and sunny or eighty degrees and sunny. (Fahrenheit, of course. Fortunately, climate change hasn't pushed California's weather *that far* in centigrade. Yet?) In any case, I knew nothing of the food I ate daily nor what it was like to develop a relationship with land—other than to recreate on it.

I figured that, if I wanted to be a responsible reader of biblical texts, I needed to immerse myself in agricultural work to have a better grasp of the seasonal festivals, vegetal metaphors, and herbal allusions strewn through this literature. And so, I made the "wise" decision to work full-time on a farm while also beginning a master's degree in theological studies. Well, it was a wise decision for my personal and spiritual growth, not to mention agricultural knowledge, but it was, without doubt, a foolish move for my finances.

I won't bore you with the details of routine crop-care, tiresome harvests, and unruly livestock. Nor will I detail the financial pressures that accompany managing an organic, community-supported agriculture (CSA) operation in an age of agribusiness. But I will tell you that, after a few seasons bouncing between farms while doing my best to curry the favor of my professors, I met Judy.

Judy was easily the most skilled grower I had met while farming. She still is, I think. Judy is one of the head farmers of one of the longest-running CSAs in New Jersey, which has been operating for about as long as I have been alive. Despite her wisdom and tenacious grit—words she'd object to me using to depict her—Judy called herself a "gardener." She still does, in fact.

Some thirty-plus years of full-time farming and she calls herself a "gardener," because, according to her, "farmers" are the people who taught her, the folks she looks up to—still. Nothing about this is "performative." She's serious, and I believe her.

Judy's been faithfully working that same plot of land for several decades alongside a crew of steadfast, driven growers. The amount of people they have fed in those years is unthinkable. Their partnership with each other and the more-than-human world makes this possible.

But if there's one thing that even Judy would claim as her own, it's her kale.[1] For some thirty years, Judy has been saving kale seed.

Year after year, Judy has saved seed from the heartiest, sweetest kale they grow on the farm—processing, drying, and storing its seed for the seasons to come.

This kale is nothing short of a paradox: it thrives in the cold, which makes it sweeter than you can imagine; it does not harden itself to the frost but instead stays tender. Who among us could say this is true of ourselves?

I mostly enjoy kale in the same way that most other folks also pretend to, but I *love* Judy's kale. It's remarkable not just because it is flavorsome but because it tastes of care. For several decades, in a quiet corner of New Jersey (which is not an oxymoron, I assure you), a woman has been quietly performing alchemy: tying her senses to seed to entice sweetness out of the soil.

Judy's kale exists as an act of faith. She might not call it that. But I would. It would not be but for her persistent care and enduring commitment. And it will not exist in perpetuity unless others follow her in this work. But, even still, Judy's kale will continue to change, evolving in partnership with shifting seasons and the unpredictabilities that they bring.

Maybe Judy's right: we never are farmers but are only ever *becoming* so. So it seems that Judy's kale, too, is not "final." It is ongoing. Becoming sweeter. More tender. We don't arrive. We remain in process. At least if we know what to look for. If we, like Judy, give ourselves over to the act of faithful tending.

⌀

Those Who Come Before

Seed-saving is straightforward in meaning. The name tells you all you need to know. Mostly.

Seed-saving refers to the process of growing plants for particular characteristics and then gathering and storing their seed for eventual sowing. Humans have done this for millennia.

The crops that we currently think of as crops have not always been as they are. Tomatoes were *tiny* jungle fruit. Bananas were squat things without much, well, "banana" in them at all. And God only knows that the devilish hot peppers that now wreck our GI tracts were not always the pain-inducing phenomenon we know them as today.

What we call and consider crops are the confluence of eco-systemic attributes, climatic trends, and caring hands. The seeds from crops are the outgrowth of the partnership of places, peoples, and plants. They don't appear on their own, because nothing ever appears on its own. No plant is an island. Everything is intercon-nected.

Of course, when you bring genetically modified seeds into the conversation, then it's a different story. That sort of work is not collaborative so much as it is invasive and intrusive.[2]

So, needless to say, when I speak of seed-saving as a practice, I mean the process of stewarding seeds in ways that are bioregion-specific, culturally attuned, biodiverse, organic, non-GMO, nonproprietary, and so on. By seed-saving, I mean the small-scale work of preserving seeds that are aligned with one's ecosystemic qualities, community needs, culinary interests, and the like. A number of other qualifications could be added here, but I trust this is clarification enough.

Seeds are *storied.* They themselves are the story of time, climate, landscape, critters, and more. They carry memories with them: genealogical histories melding weather patterns, insect encounters, tasty meals, and so forth. By saving seeds, we enable them to tell and retell their story. They incarnate a millennial legacy of sprout-ing, growing, flowering, fruiting, wilting.

Seeds bear the story of death and resurrection—unending. Even the Christian parable of death and resurrection as embodied in the ritual of the Eucharist isn't possible without the labor of wheat and grape seeds.

Seeds bear the story of the hands of the seed-keepers who have caressed, plucked, winnowed, dried, cradled. They bear the trace of *those who have come before.*

Seed-saving is the stewardship of memory—time stretched through places, peoples, plants.

And, thus, it seems to be the case that the agency of seed-savers can be in service of honoring those who came before or erasing our interconnected pasts. It unveils the ways in which our activities can ground us in relationship to our context—ecological, political, familial—or can divorce us from the flows of entangled life.

∽

Anti-Extraction

Where does value come from? How do we ascribe value? Should we have that kind of authority to ascribe value? Who is even included in that "we"?

I don't know about you, but I find myself believing some pretty harmful lies about this stuff all the time. One example: I am hard on myself when I prioritize my wellness over my work, because I feel like my work makes my life valuable. Anything other than sheer productivity in my work leads to all kinds of self-doubt, if not self-loathing.

In the process of writing this very book, I've had days where I just couldn't . . . write.

If you've ever written anything at all, you know that sometimes when you sit down to write, it doesn't just always happen. When I try to describe this experience to my friends or even to you here-now, it sometimes feels like writing is a form of magic or wizardry or something like that—like writing is somehow "beyond" me. But it really does feel that way sometimes: my best days of writing feel a lot more like getting out of the way of myself and *letting the writing happen.* It feels much more like a "letting be" than a gritting or producing. If writing is anything at all, it's about flowing. Letting the words *move through* you. Letting the language *move* you. Maybe it's a little like the experience that some might describe as "feeling the Spirit."

Needless to say, there have been more days than I'd like to admit—and I mean *entire days*—where I've tried to write and just . . . nothing. The anguish I feel on those unproductive days is difficult to describe. It's easy to spiral: Am I lazy? Do I not care about this work? Am I letting down my students, family, and friends who have supported me in my pursuits? Why can't I just *write*?

When I am living up to the values I claim to hold, I have the wherewithal to realize that this struggle seems to be a normal part of the writing process—at least for every person I know who writes—but that, also, much of the anguish I feel is from my belief in the great lie of capitalism: my value is derived from—and *can only* be derived from—my productivity. I am good only insofar as I am an efficient, effective worker. And my labor, my time, and my energy are only valuable insofar as they produce profit of some sort. So, even if I am productive, but my productivity is utilized on a task that is not profitable—like, say, reading an influential novel—this effort is still "valueless." What a joke. As soon as you say it aloud, you realize its absurdity, never mind its inherent ableism.[3]

Yes, work is good. Labor is part of a life well-lived, in my opinion. But, by labor, I mean the labor of artistic expression and community-building and intellectual inquiry and agricultural cultivation and play. Not to mention the labor of love. To note the importance of labor is far from advocating for the absolute sacrifice of one's life from 9 a.m. to 5 p.m., Monday to Friday, from ages sixteen to sixty-five-plus. How telling it is that one of the first questions you're asked in the United States when meeting someone is, "What do you do?" by which they mean, "What is your job and therefore your identity?"

Capitalistic value is absurd because it has nothing to do with *intrinsic* value. It has everything to do with *extractive* value. Capitalistic value is only that which can be extracted: whether labor from a person, lumber from an oak, or hydroelectric energy from a river.

This is why capitalism and the ways it has shaped our society—not least our universities—can hardly comprehend the *intrinsic* good of art and literature and music and dance and so on.

While our economic paradigm has convinced us that we cannot rest without feelings of guilt nor adequately account for the intrinsic value of friendship or honeybees or experimental art or public spaces or sunrises, by what alternative means might we derive and define value? Must it be the case that value solely emerges from scarcity—the less of something there is, the more valuable it becomes?

Seeds refuse to abide by this logic.

Seeds constitute a multiplying of possibility, thereby shirking economies of scarcity. That is, seed-saving generates value out of the possibility of abundance, not lack. A single cayenne pepper plant, for example, can yield up to eighty peppers, each pepper containing many dozens of seeds, and each seed, under appropriate storage conditions, is viable for several years (and sometimes a few decades). Proliferation doesn't yet begin to describe these processes. The evolutionary design of seeds to travel by wind or animal unveils the persistence of plants. And "volunteers"—the agricultural term for crops that appear on their own, not intentionally planted by the grower—that appear in the compost pile or garden bed from last year's crop remind us that seeds' potentiality can flourish without human care, too.

Seeds remind us that scarcity is manufactured.

Lest it need to be said, the emergent bounty that is unleashed by responsible seed-saving practices should not be mistaken as an argument for limitless expansion and boundless growth, as proponents of capitalism would like us to think. These lies, as we know, externalize and abstract Earth and its inhabitants. Put simply, capitalism excludes context from its equation: logging corporations never consider the toll clear-cutting takes on topsoil stability; agribusinesses fail to acknowledge the costs of synthetic fertilizer application in creating aquifer death zones through excessive runoff; fracking operations routinely avoid accountability for contaminating drinking water. It's only ever about what can be extracted—never what collateral damage emerges in the wake of extraction.

Value must be neither extractive nor abstracted. Seed-saving inspires an entirely different mindset.

∽

Tuning In to Place

What precisely is the work of seed-saving then? How might it redefine value as such?

There, perhaps, could be a narrowness by which the practice is defined: human mastery over vegetal life, eugenically determining what will continue and what will perish. Is seed-saving but another self-serving human-interest project? Simply deeming that which is valuable as only what is valuable for us?

As it happens, whatever possibilities persist for meaningful human community amid climate catastrophe, none will be possible without seeds. Hope cannot be made without seeds.

But seeds are not a panacea, given that they are thoroughly particular. There is no one seed that rules them all, and any such thinking will almost certainly lead to devastation, as invasive species often do.

Of course, invasive species are not inherently bad. They are simply *out of place.* That is, the value they bring and the contributions they make to their ecosystemic origins are outsized when out of place. They tip the balance, disrupt relational equilibria, and untie the webs that make up bioregions. They do not find right relation because they are out of relation to place from the start.

As context changes, what is good also changes.

What is good isn't relativistic so much as it is *relational.* Love, too, is this way: there is no one way to love; we do not each embody and accept love in the same ways; our expressions of love shift over time and differ depending on context. Love is not relativistic—it's not whatever we want it to be. It's relational: in relationship to particular persons at particular times in particular contexts. This is always the case.

Thus, to express love for the ecological in efforts of faithful justice-seeking must necessarily differ with context. As agrarian Wendell Berry argues, "The land is too various in its kinds, climates, conditions, declivities, aspects, and histories to conform to any *generalized understanding* or to prosper under *generalized treatment*."[4] What works in one place may not—often *will not*—work in another. What is good here may not be—often *is not*—good there.

Seeds help us consider value as bioregional. They remind that value does not exist in the abstract.

Value emerges from context: a hammer is useless if the context demands a screwdriver; a lecture I'd give my college students wouldn't work with a bunch of kindergartners; a fish doesn't do so well without water. Context matters, and context helps us understand value. Hence, there is no panacea to our planetary crisis.[5] Any such thinking stems from a capitalistic worldview that can never recognize that value is only ever placed, particular, cultural.

The regenerative capacities of seeds demand that our attention mind the ground and tend to place. Externalization is not possible in this process. Neither is abstraction. Seeds are only ever grown somewhere and can only ever be grown somewhere. This, too, is obvious as soon as you say it. But by this, I mean that their value is only ever in relation and in context.

There is no valuation outside of relation, seeds remind.

Further, the regenerative capacities of seeds turn our attention from that of extraction to that of laboring in place—at least when we save seeds mindfully. What exactly happens in the process of seed-saving?

Seed-saving embodies a radical gathering. Seed-saving is collaborative through and through and all the way down. This collaboration exceeds the simple fact that seed-saving occurs only through human and botanical interactivity, wherein the human partners with plants to selectively cultivate and grow crops for the traits that they desire. Further, and more compellingly, the process of saving seeds extends the scope of the communal, as such, beyond this human-plant partnership.

By saving seeds, we not only co-labor with plants, nor do we—if wise—only save seeds for the selection of traits desirable for human survival. Yes, this happens, and it's especially crucial to do so for cultures and communities whose culinary traditions, religious meals, agricultural practices, and collective gatherings have been ignored, erased, blockaded, bulldozed, and bombed. Responsible seed-saving can function as a crucial form of liberative reclamation, fostering food sovereignty through seed sovereignty.

Crucially, the partnership embodied in seed-saving extends far beyond our relations with the vegetal or botanical. It allows for the mindful partnering of that which engenders life and its ongoing possibility for the plant, as well as the soil, pollinator, watershed, ecosystem, and human critter alike. The mindful cultivation of crops enables the consideration and bolstering of soil stability, pollinator presence, water consumption, ecosystem balance, and more with the plant partner.

To tend plants and, with care, steward their seeds accentuates the nature of our toil as always only ever bioregional and placed. The scope of our gathering thus proliferates and deepens: it becomes rooted in place. Our stewarding of seeds unfolds possibilities to factor the winged, webbed, watery, and beyond in our decision-making.

Seed-saving pushes us to extend the mandate to "love one's neighbor" to one's *more-than-human neighbors*.

This does not mean that we won't, in the words of philosopher Thom Van Dooren, be "required to take a stand for some possible worlds and not others."[6] Of course that's the case. Still, seed-saving suggests the possibility of valuation as reciprocal, regenerative, renewing exchange.

Seed-saving bears the promise of reframing value bioregionally. This could sound an awful lot like glamorizing our environmental relations, glossing over the fact that it is only ever through the death of something that allows our life (at least, strictly speaking, when it comes to our eating). Instead, though, I hope you hear this suggested paradigm of regenerative labor as an extension of Robin Wall Kimmerer's argument that we must stop thinking of "sustainability" as "how much can we take and still get away with" and, instead, must reframe this Western, colonial worldview to account for faithful environmental justice as not only how and what we take but, crucially, *what we give*.[7]

Seed-saving affords us one such possibility of reconceiving hopeful labor as contextual, cooperative, and complementary.

Amid a changing climate, seed-saving forces us to reckon with the reality that our gathering for the sake of justice and liberation is incomplete—indeed *impossible*—without considering *where* we gather. What's more, seed-saving expands our consideration of who is part of this gathering—disclosing that hopeful gathering cannot be limited only to the human.

We cannot care for the Earth as if it were one thing. We can only care for particular places—multitudinous and multiplex. By keeping seeds, we keep alive the stories of those who came before—human, humic, aquatic, botanical, insectile, and so many others in our ecological webs.

⌘

Seeding Hope

My clammy palm mimics a bowl as I cradle dozens of kernels. It's tempting to think of these seeds as inert. Or, if alive, as pre-programmed.

They are actual. They indeed exist. They *are*, yet they are simultaneously *not yet*.

I've come to realize that these seeds are so much more about *potentiality* than *actuality.* They are *potentiality itself.* Sheer promise, no guarantee. Seeds are nothing if not persistent faith.

Soil nurtured a plant into good health. A plant, in collaboration with its climate and context, willed its seeds into being. And a farmer—in this case, my partner—collected, dried, and stored them, persistently. All this is preceded by eons of evolution, climatic trends, bioregional shifts, and the like.

None of these histories are found on seed packets. At least not from any major corporation these days. At most you will find germination rate, spacing, planting depth, days to harvest, and such—their wisdom reduced to computational projections, not to mention a copyright or trademark. This is helpful, to a degree. It's fine; it's just not the whole picture.

As exemplifications of hope, these okra seeds in my palm are meaningless in the abstract. They matter not without context: in this case, healthy soil within which to rest.

The mustard seed of faith means nothing without the community of wind, carbon, earthworm, sun, and rain to nurture it. The collaborative work of faith is nothing short of a holy communion.

Maybe then, the clouds themselves might join our cloud of witnesses.

∽

How to Save Pepper Seeds

It hardly gets any easier than saving pepper seeds.

Select a pepper of your choice: ideally one that seems healthy, strong, and with the characteristics you're looking for—whether color, shape, sweetness, spiciness, or the like.

Cut it open, and scrape out the seeds onto a plate. If any seeds still have some of the whiteish pith on them, gently remove it so that the seeds are separate and bare.

Spread the seeds on the plate and leave them to dry for at least 5–7 days. Jostle them every so often so that both sides of the seed dry. Seeds should be dry in a week if left in roughly 40% humidity. As long as they're not in a super humid environment, they'll dry just fine, even if it takes a bit longer than a week.

Once dry, store them in a sealed container of some sort (glass jar, seed packet, etc.) in a cool and dry place. You'll probably want to label them with the variety, year, or other information you think will be helpful for future identification and growing. You don't have to, but you might end up with a lot of "mystery peppers" that you'll have to taste-test eventually.

Your taste buds will probably thank you for sparing them multiple raw hot peppers.

Fermenting

Processing Peppers

The jar is cloudy and kind of gross.

It has a film stretched across the surface, made lumpy from the red chunks pressing against it. I'm not sure if the liquid is more tan or gray, but it's not visually appealing and certainly isn't appetizing. But soon it'll be food—or, really, a condiment. At least, I'm trusting that it will.

We grew too many hot peppers this year. The dry heat from a rather rainless summer—perhaps now the norm—was perfect for the peppers, of which we planted more than needed out of fear that they'd struggle like last year. We were wrong, and now I have a massive jar of diced peppers fermenting on my counter. And this jar isn't even the first. Hardly.

This is a good problem to have if you love hot sauce. And I do. But having mostly only made dehydrated peppers or salsa in seasons past, I've been a bit daunted by the fear of taking on a new fermentation project, and the cloudy, chunky jar is only amplifying my concerns.

But, like all else, fermentation is an act of faith.

Yes, I gleaned knowledge from experts. I consulted those with experience and followed their guidance. I don't think just winging it would be good for my GI system. But, regardless of expertise, you can't force fermentation to happen. You can't force transformation. You can only cultivate the conditions in which fermentation is possible.

So, each morning, I look at the cloudy, chunky jar with disgust and delight. It challenges my perception of what is good, never mind edible. And, in a week, when the slurry is blended with vinegar and cooked down a bit, it'll glow—*aflame* both in color and flavor. It'll be anything but disgusting, dashed across all kinds of dishes.

But, for now, it's cloudy and kind of gross. And I will be patient. But I'll probably hide it in a cabinet when guests come over.

⁊

Material Fermentation

Kimchi. Pickles. Sauerkraut. Beer. Cheese. Kefir. Mirin. Vinegar. Miso. Tempeh. Wine. Fermentation is responsible for all of these delights and so many more.

Fermentation refers to the various processes of anaerobic metabolization by bacteria and other microorganisms, creating the zesty flavors, as well as rich nutrients, of countless alimentary innovations.

Fermentation processes yield a multitude of results, including carbon dioxide (e.g., leavened bread), ethanol (e.g., wine), lactic acid (e.g., cheese), and more. Another benefit of fermentation is the reduction of phytic acid, an antinutrient that inhibits our bodies' absorption of key minerals such as iron, calcium, and zinc.

Our taste buds seem to light up in response to fermented foods—sharp, acidic, pungent—sometimes with bliss and at other times aversion. Fermentation yields tangy tastes that often far extend the preservation and shelf life of foodstuffs.

But fermentation is more than all of this.

Metaphoric Fermentation

Fermentation simultaneously transforms both cuisine *and* culture.

As Sandor Ellix Katz, a fermentation expert, writes, "The English language uses the word *fermentation* to describe not only the literal phenomenon of cellular metabolism that it is—microorganisms and their enzymes digesting and transforming nutrients—but also much more broadly to indicate a state of agitation, excitement, and bubbliness."[1] English preserves an interconnection between the material flavor and metaphorical fervor of fermentation. And Katz's work to evangelize the good news of fermented foods seeks to transform ingredients and ideologies.

Following Katz's urge to consider "fermentation as metaphor," might we uncover novel ways to conceive of—indeed incarnate— a radical transformation of our world? What might *noticing* the material-metaphoric interconnectedness of fermentation yield in how we *gather*?

Katz describes metaphoric fermentation as the experience of getting "caught up in a feeling of shared effervescence" and as "an unstoppable force that people everywhere have harnessed, and gotten caught up in, in all sorts of ways."[2] Katz continues,

> Fermentation can be driven by hopes, dreams, and desires; or by necessity, desperation, and anger; or by other forces altogether. Fermentation is always going on somewhere, though generally not everywhere. Sometimes in its absence it can seem elusive. But when metaphorical fermentation occurs, it often spreads, *transforming what was into what's next. Fermentation is no less than an engine of social change.*[3]

Given the precariousness of our planet and all its inhabitants— but especially those long marginalized by patriarchy, capitalism, homophobia, and racism—Katz contends, "Now more than ever, we need the bubbling transformative power of fermentation."[4] Thus, Katz suggests that fermentation can serve as "a form of activism." Materially, it offers practical and practicable ways to resist an industrialized food system that overwhelmingly pollutes, depletes nutrients, and wastes countless goods; fermentation proffers the capacity for localizing practices that can build communities.[5] And metaphorically, fermentation invites us to rethink our worldview altogether.

coʃ

Fermented Imagination

Fermentation happens by means of *collaboration*, not control.

One must cooperate with bacteria and archaea to create conditions for the possibility of fermentation, but one cannot control it, per se. There is no forcing fermentation. Instead, we must attune ourselves to the matrices that make life possible in order to participate in processes of fermentation.

As Katz notes, "Fermentation is a force that cannot be controlled, and the changes it renders are not always desirable."[6] It's a relationship. It's something we tap into.

Fermentation is the process of gathering with the more-than-human world in potent, if sometimes unseen, ways. Through fermentation, we participate in something powerful—but *not* because it's something we have power "over." It's an *empowering* kind of power—not an *overpowering* one.

Fermentation adheres *not* to the classically masculinist traditions of power as "control"—in the ways many theologians have depicted the divine—but instead suggests a queer, feminist, relational power as "empowerment." This power is neither domineering nor surveilling. Instead, it's *among, with, alongside.*

And we can take these revelations into all of our other relations and our conceptions thereof—not least of the divine.[7]

coʃ

Impure Thoughts

Fermentation *harnesses* potentiality, *partnering* with possibility. It can be neither arrested nor subjugated, although it can be *cultivated* and *affected.*

And this is only possible because, in Katz's words, our "existential context is a microbial matrix . . . a vast matrix of intertwining life-forms at different scales, interacting, mutually coexisting, and feeding off one another."[8] We're caught up in a web of creatures and forces and animacies—apparent and concealed. This carries consequence, however. It demands our recognition that, as Katz puts it, "We can no longer imagine [microorganisms] as our mortal enemies to be destroyed by any means necessary. Instead, we must recognize them as partners."[9] In the same way that compost helps us reimagine our understanding of change and conversion, fermentation reorients our definition of community.

We are naught but the product of microorganisms.

A great deal of what makes up a human being is, in fact, "nonhuman." We breathe wind and drink rain and consume sun—yes, indirectly, but also quite materially. We exist by virtue of the terrestrial relations in which we are interwoven. Moreover, and pertinent to the subject of fermentation, we are hosts to microorganisms of all kinds—which enable our own life! A significant portion of the cells in our body, as it happens, are nonhuman cells.[10]

Katz states, "We come from bacteria, in a long-term evolutionary way; we live among them and viruses and many other microorganisms; and we depend upon them for functionality and survival." We live in a "sort of microbial force field, a complex community of bacteria, viruses, fungi, and other organisms that live upon and within us."[11] This is undeniable. But the ethical, ecological, and theological consequences of this force field emerge in Katz's next claim: "If purity means a state devoid of contamination, that is pure fantasy."[12]

When taken seriously, fermentation radically alters our perceptions of what is good, clean, right, righteous, safe. It upends our notions of boundaries and belonging.

Fermentation unveils the fundamental porosity of the world.

Nothing is bounded, impermeable, or impassable. *Porosity* enables life: breath, photosynthesis, precipitation, digestion, and much more are only possible because of permeability.

I know that it's easy to think in terms of neat edges, tidy boundaries, clear limits. I, too, have been instructed to think of impen-
etrable borders between human/animal, nature/culture, spirit/flesh,
us/them, and so on. But that we might prefer to think in these
terms does not mean that this is how our world, in fact, *is*. What
if, as revealed to us by the fizzy activity of fermentation, we allowed
our imaginations to bubble by allowing for a bit more porosity?

When we tear down these ideological walls, we can see a new
horizon.

Of course, all I'm really suggesting here is that we let our bio-
logical and ecological realities inspire our ethical and theological
thinking a bit more than we may presently allow. I'm proposing
that we break open the binaries of in/out, pure/impure, clean/dirty,
heaven/earth, and on. The cloudy, chunky liquid of my fermenting hot peppers confronts me with this breaking open of binaries:
what I've been taught to treat with disgust is, in fact, caught up in
a process of rich and transformative *life*.

Fermentation seeks not purity so much as collaborative community. Fermentation is impossible without things that we traditionally conceive of as contaminants—yeasts, molds, bacteria, and so
forth. Katz affirms, "Food is never clean. Food is never pure. Food
always involves ingesting other forms of life. Unintended smaller
forms of life are inevitably there, too."[13] Yes, there are forms of
these things—that is, yeasts, molds, and so on—that can produce
undesired, even quite harmful, results in a batch of kraut or beer
or kimchi or the like. Culinary safety remains paramount. But
neither our theological nor political nor culinary imaginations
can minimize the vital importance of these microbial beings and
their functions.

Purity politics has no place in this beloved community.

As Katz argues, "Far from contamination, the presence of microorganisms in cohesive structured communities is a powerful
force of equilibrium, playing a protective and regulating role, in

our intestines, in the soil, and on the Earth as a whole."[14] We are coconspirators with the unseen in all aspects of our lives; fermentation just makes it evident.

Fermentation is communal through and through, expanding the bounds of the beloved community to the invisible-to-the-naked-eye life-forms that pervade our planetary existence. And, insofar as we recognize our indebtedness not just to each other but to the multitudinous more-than-human kin that bolster our lives, we open new paths to practice love and sustainability—the two *now entangled indiscreetly.*

As anthropologist Mercedes Villalba beautifully conveys, "What fermentation shows us is the invisible connections of everything. Bubbling life unlocked in things that are hidden from us by the opacity of matter."[15] By practicing fermentation, "you learn to cultivate the future."[16]

Through fermentation, we are participating in something miraculous. We are invited into collaborative work that ultimately nourishes—both body and spirit.

Fermentation isn't strictly material *or* metaphoric. It's existential. Our entire existence hinges on the matrix of life that makes fermentation possible.

Fermentation is but the *celebration thereof.*

∽

A Play in Three Acts

Act One

My forearms ache. You'd think after a decade of rock climbing that wouldn't be the case.

But cabbage is tough, apparently. I'm astounded by this with every batch of sauerkraut that I make.

I grab a fistful of shredded leaves and squeeze. Handful after handful, the leaves soften and begin to produce liquid. I don't know how to describe the feeling of cabbage juice squishing through your fingers without it sounding totally off-putting. It's really not—each drop a tactile gratitude that few other culinary practices offer.

It's remarkable what a pinch of salt and a few minutes of effort can do. I commune with a life force that I hadn't known was there—or at least never gave any real thought to.

Another handful. Another wonder.

Act Two

My friend Jeff, a minister and something of a mystic, recently rescued a fancy Swiss coffee maker, gifted by a neighbor who thought it was defunct. They'd tried to get it to work but—nothing.

But Jeff's handy and likes coffee, so he figured he'd give it a shot. A few quick tests and some button-pressing and—*voilà*—he got it running again.

On my last visit to his home, he *insisted* on making my partner and me coffee in the morning. But not just "coffee." Oh no. Rather, *cosmic coffee*.

I didn't know what to expect.

The following morning:

"You know how the Milky Way undulates and flows? The ways in which our galaxy pulses with waves?" Jeff asked—jubilant.

"Yeah, I suppose," I answered, unsure. (I checked. He's right.[17])

"Well, this coffee is like our galaxy. It drifts and surges like the cosmos."

The machine buzzed and churned and sputtered. I watched with the skepticism of a nonbeliever. (I'm telling you my cosmic coffee conversion story, after all.)

Some hissing and a bit of steam, and into a glass mug poured a frothy coffee, rich hickory with ivory foam drifting above.

We brought our eyes level with the countertop—our backs bent, almost prayerfully.

"Look! Do you see it?" Jeff inquired.

Like the pulse of something ancient and unknown, the coffee indeed undulated in almost indescribable ways. Where the foam met the coffee, spirals and whirls and eddies pulsating like the cosmos.

It was actually the most beautiful cup of coffee I've seen.

But, at the end of the day, it *was* just another cup of coffee. Another morning's beverage, the likely result of some remarkable global, capitalistic story and vast carbon footprint. I know. I get it.

But this story's not about coffee or even cosmic coffee. Not in the least.

It's about Jeff, who knows to look for God in all things, who seeks the face of the divine in the most mundane of circumstances and sees Earth in *awesome* wonder—turning this skeptic into a believer.

Act Three

I watch my sauerkraut fizz.

I laugh when it overflows onto the counter. Its activity can't be contained—*Leuconostoc mesenteroides* producing carbon dioxide before *Lactobacillus brevis* and *Lactobacillus plantarum* yield tangy lactic acid.

I look with delight at the impossible fact that putting stuff in a jar for just a few days can produce something delectable, indeed nourishing. And it's not something "I" made. It takes a village (of bacteria) to make sauerkraut.

I lift the jar up, letting light from the window illuminate this microcosmic effervescence.

Inside, a miracle only possible because this Earth is no less than a "communion of subjects,"[18] is nothing other than a "covenant of reciprocity."[19]

When we commune faithfully with each other—with *every* "other"—a thread of love can be found in all things.

Even cabbage.

⟨⟩

Simple Fermentation

Beets. Quite the divisive root vegetable, I know.

Either you love them or you hate them. (Unless we're talking about those canned, squiggly cut beets that you find in a salad bar, which ought to be universally hated.)

Whether you love or hate beets, one of the simplest ways to practice fermentation is by making *beet kvass*.

Beet kvass is a lacto-fermented drink. The naturally occurring lactic-acid-producing bacteria (typically of the genus *Lactobacillus*) found on beets will break down the beets' sugars.

Think of it as a natural soda. It's like an earthier-tasting kombucha that's a beautiful hue of purple.

How do you make it? Easy!

1. Cut one or two beets into one-inch (ish) chunks.
2. Put the cut beets in water—maybe a liter or so.
3. Add a pinch of salt.
4. Close the jar with a lid and wait.

Like many other fermented foods, you will likely need to open the jar every so often—maybe once a day or every other day—to release the gas created during fermentation.

Taste the kvass throughout the process until it's to your liking. I usually let mine ferment for a week or two, depending on the temperature in my home. Once it's ready, strain it and refrigerate.

Experiment! Scale up the recipe. Add lemon or ginger or herbs or more. Try a secondary ferment to carbonate the kvass. The possibilities are endless.

You can make all kinds of natural sodas using this same lacto-fermentation process with many other ingredients: strawberry kvass, raspberry kvass, watermelon kvass, oh my!

From here, you can branch out to try other things like brewing kombucha, making a ginger bug, using kefir grains, and more.

Ferment your heart out (metaphorically).

Cycling

Insurgency

Revolutions. Not the bold, audacious ones. Those are coming.
Sweat. Breath. Wind. Ground. One.
Revolutions. Quiet and not quite finished. Each, yes, dovetailing
into the next. There is neither beginning nor end. Only revolutions.
Cadence. Stamina. Power. Posture. Many.
Revolutions. All the world's *not* a stage. Not a backdrop. Not a
set. All the world's a revolving. A spinning. A becoming. Cyclical
is the shape of the ecological. Spirals—fractals all the way down.
All the world's not a stage. It's a Möbius strip.

Maybe this is all too contrived. Maybe I'm getting ahead of
myself. How interesting, though, that most of contemporary life
is ahead of itself. Future-oriented. Goal-oriented. Forget the Now.
The Future beckons.

There's nothing worse in a revolution than getting ahead of
oneself. The temptation of some Promised Land blurs perceptions
of the present. Trying to be "there" when one is inescapably *here*.
But what is the present without the tantalizing lures of *what-
could-yet-be*?

The question becomes not how far we are willing to go. The
question becomes *how far we ought to go*.
Revolutions. The only Way.

⌁

The Simplicity and Mystery of Cycling

Bicycles operate by means of revolution. Of the crankset. Of the wheelset. Of the mindset.

Legs turn cranks turn wheels. But, despite being rather simple machines in theory, bicycles are a conundrum even to physicists and engineers.

Push a riderless bike fast enough and not only will it stay upright, but, when shoved from the side, it'll adjust gyroscopically to self-correct, remaining upright. How does this actually work? No one really knows.[1] The *variables* of this phenomenon are known: turnability of the front wheel, steering axis, tire contact point, caster effect, and gyroscopic effect of the spinning wheels, among other matters.[2] But how exactly these variables relate to one another and interact remains something of a mystery. Even whether some of these variables are necessary—including ones like the caster effect and gyroscopic effect, which have long been deemed the "reason" that bikes even work—is now up in the air.[3]

The phrase "It's as easy as riding a bicycle" evidently does not apply to bicycle physics.

Still, even if it's unclear how they work, bikes are quite simple machines—at least when held in contrast to artificial intelligence, large language models, quantum computing, and the like. Circles. Triangles. Rubber. Steel. Energy. Motion.

The simplicity of a cycle[4] makes it endlessly versatile and adaptable: cycles come in dozens of shapes to be accessible to persons of nearly all ages, abilities, sizes, capacities, and more. Upright bikes, recumbent bikes, tricycles, hand cycles, adaptive cycles: cycling takes countless forms, all of which yield *movement*. (Let's exclude stationary bikes for now for the sake of the argument.) And the movement catalyzed by the cycle is both spatial and political: the bicycle played no small role in the women's suffrage movement in the United States, not to mention the transformation of femme fashion.[5]

What's more, the bicycle is also the most efficient human-powered mode of transportation. The same energy output used to walk (around three miles per hour) achieves ten to fifteen miles per hour on a standard bike.[6] Whereas a person walking at an average pace for a given distance consumes energy at a rate of .75 calorie per gram per kilometer, a person on a bike consumes only .15 per calorie per gram per kilometer.[7] Since bikes can—at least in some circumstances—achieve 99 percent mechanical efficiency, it's difficult to imagine a more efficient, and thus sustainable, means of moving.

So, yes, this mysterious technology is fairly green, fairly accessible, and thus good for reducing emissions, but beyond this, how might cycling offer a parable for community building amid planetary precarity? How might cycling reshape how our communities *gather* and move amid climate crisis?

⌁

For most of our existence as a species, the scale of human life has been incredibly local. Tiny. Minute. Limited to a village or, perhaps, in some cases, a small region. And, if a large region due to transhumance—that is, a seasonal pattern of movement, more predictable than that of "nomadic pastoralism"—then only slowly, over extended durations of time.

Prior to industrialization and the transportation technologies it facilitated, the scope of human existence was quite small. This is not to say that peoples haven't traveled, moved routinely and nomadically, or migrated great distances. Of course, this is true. And some of the most fascinating bits of human history, in my opinion, come from the tenacity that peoples display in the movements they undertake. But, on the whole, the spatial scale at which a person lived was generally quite small compared to today.

Post-railway and now, especially, post–air travel, the scale of human life has multiplied to unthinkable levels. The relative accessibility of these tools coupled with the globalizing technologies of the digital world have expanded the very dimensional range of life itself.

There is a *too-much-ness* about contemporary life that is facilitated by social media, global capitalism, and rapid transit.

The scale of life today is global—at the expense of particular places.

Never have humans had access to this magnitude of information and opportunity. And, thus, never have humans had to bear the weight of the world in such an overwhelming way. What I mean is that, what most of us feel that we are "expected" to "pay attention to" is so unbelievably massive in scale, it is impossible to hold it all. Perhaps you experience this overwhelm when you read the news or scroll through digital media. I surely do. And what exactly does this reveal? That which I feel compelled to care about far exceeds my capacity for care. I can't hold it all. It's simply too much. This is the brutal consequence of global interconnectivity.

I'm not recommending callousness as a response to tragedies like genocide in Gaza or wildfires in Canada or famine in Sudan. How could I? But, at the same time, I also know that my own time, skills, resources, and energies are finite. Ethics are always a matter of prioritization, and there are times when I must prioritize some matters over others. This is the painful catch-22 of contemporary life: I wish to bear witness to the many sins of our age and seek loving responses thereto, but I simply cannot do so because of my own finitude. The world is so big, and I am so small.

The cruel irony here is that the expectation to pay attention to what's happening in the world often comes at the expense of *paying attention to the very places we inhabit.* By paying attention to "more," it seems that we're actually paying *less* attention. Or, rather, and perhaps more truthfully, the quality of our attention and the care it inspires diminish. Or at the very least it's stretched entirely *too thin.* Hence the paradox that humans' supposed knowledge is increasing as *that same knowledge* destroys the very mechanisms that support life.

The pursuit of "objective knowledge" detaches us from our environs, and thus, in the words of ecophilosopher Bruno Latour, "we have begun to see less and less of what is happening on Earth."[8] Our constructions of knowledge itself—which is to say, what is listened to and deemed authoritative—have separated humans from animals, spirit from flesh, subject from object, and knower from known. And maybe, too, heavenly from earthly. Regardless of our good intentions to know the world in order to love it, we have paid attention to the universal at the expense of the *local,* the global to the detriment of the *terrestrial.*

And this is true not only ecologically but also politically. It could very well be the case that, for many of us, the effort to stay apprised on global concerns blinds us to our local interconnections with those problems. For example, my concern about genocide happening in Gaza may actually make me miss the fact that the US government, to which I belong as a citizen, gave at least $12.5 billion in military aid[9] to Israel—not to mention dozens of F-15 fighter jets and around fourteen thousand MK-84 *one-ton* bombs[10]—just in the eight months following the war that began in October 2023.

Maybe there's something to the whole "think globally, act locally" refrain.

What if it were the case that, by paying attention to less, I was, in fact, paying attention to more? This is quite an ambiguous turn of phrase, really, as it relies on the vagueness of "less" and "more," playing with the intentional clouding of quality and quantity and their interrelation. It is perhaps clearer to say that, by paying attention to less (quantitatively speaking), we are able to pay attention to more (qualitatively speaking). But it's less fun to say it that way.

At what scale can the human operate—and *well?* Not to mention healthily? How can a person navigating globalizing economic forces

and international diplomatic happenings and close-to-home problems and neighborhood developments balance these commitments?
Is such a thing possible? If being mindful of our context, indeed
bioregion, is something we seek, how far exactly are the bounds
of our context? How far must my attention extend? How far *can*
my attention extend? I wonder: Might the spinning wheels of a
cycle help us find our way back to a life that is no longer outsized?

I have no answers to these questions. Not clear ones, anyway.
Any concise answers to any of these queries would lack nuance
and depth. They'd sacrifice something or someone for the sake of
clarity. Much has been sacrificed on this altar.

Instead, I think water and its flows could help us. The concept
of the watershed is crucial here. This'll all come back to cycling,
I assure you.

Ecotheologian Cherice Bock offers this helpful definition of
the term "watershed": "A watershed is the area where all the water
falling in the region drains to a common outlet such as a stream,
lake, or river; watersheds are divided by ridgelines, the other side
of which flows to a different outlet."[11] We all live in a particular
watershed—mine, for example, being the Ohio River Valley. I
inhabit a bioregion in which all local water—somehow, eventually—flows to the Ohio River. (Now's a good moment to look up
yours if you don't already know it!)

Expanding on activist theologian Ched Myers's concept of "watershed discipleship," Bock suggests that we consider the watershed
as a way by which we might scale our ethics. She argues, "Watershed
discipleship . . . envisions the watershed as *a scalable unit of care*:
one's smallest local watershed may form around a stream in one's
neighborhood, scaling up to a larger watershed based around a
large river, and ultimately flowing out into the ocean, linking all
watersheds."[12] The scale of the watershed concentrates our attention on our locales, but it doesn't imply ignorance of the wider
network of the biosphere either. It helps us notice our place and
how our place connects to other places.

Watersheds function as a *scalable unit of care*, focusing one's attention on the local—but not at the expense of the planetary! And vice versa. As Bock reaffirms, "Thinking bioregionally encourages [persons] to become environmentally conscious by starting from their own grounded location, while being aware of their impact on the entire biosphere."[13] With this framework, we could establish an ethic at a scale that *makes sense*. The scope seems to be one that we can, in fact, *pay attention to.* Or it's at least a scope that's far more relatable and relational. The question is no longer, "How can I be a good person?" in this overwhelming and overwhelmingly massive world but instead becomes, "How can I be a good person *here?*" Something like the Golden Rule, for example, would thus translate to, "Do unto your downstream neighbors as you would have your upstream neighbors do unto you."

Water connects us all, flows through us all. Knowing how our actions impact our immediate waterways and the places to which they flow is crucial.

But it could be the case that the surging nature of water might not feel all that grounding. It establishes a sense of place that always flows somewhere else. So, while the watershed fosters a crucial sense of interdependent interconnectivity, what exactly does this mean when it comes to gathering in community and living within the rhythms of our bioregion?

After all, it can be hard to conceive of one's watershed outside of streams, hollers, basins, and rivers. If the watershed is the concave that holds this fluid life force, what of the convex? What about ridgelines and foothills and prominences, even plains? What of the areas where water does not gather but instead pours away from?

Could we supplement the ethical frame of reference that is the watershed with a complementary scalable unit of care? One that is sensible for a grounded and thus necessarily communal life?

Enter the "cycleshed."

The cycleshed—or, even more casually, the "bikeshed"—is the cycling analogue to the watershed. Urban studies researchers

Hiroyuki Iseki and Matthew Tingstrom define "bikeshed" as "a catchment area of bicycle trips or demand in relation to a single point analogous to the term, 'watershed.'"[14] We could say that the cycleshed is the area surrounding a particular point—often and most likely the place one dwells—within which a person could reasonably travel by cycle.

Imagine a roughly circular bubble that encompassed the region in which you could reasonably cycle: What if we were to live our lives at that scale? What if our communities were developed in such a way as to make this possible? What would it mean to define one's community by the distances made possible by human-powered cycling?

For most, this could not yet be actual but is instead *aspirational*. Most places in the United States, for example, are hardly walkable, let alone cyclable. The systematic divestment from public infrastructure like multiuse trails, protected bike lanes, and the like has been driven, as it were, by the motor vehicle–obsessed culture of the United States—subsidized by the coffers of fossil-fuel lobbyists and Big Oil apologists. But what if communities were created to be not only livable within the bounds of the cycleshed but *enjoyable*—indeed *pleasurable*? The cycleshed is the imagination of grounded communities whose sense of place is shaped by the range of the cycle.

The cycleshed expands the scope of so-called fifteen-minute cities—a vision of communities in which all basic needs can be acquired within a fifteen-minute walk, bike, or public transit ride[15]—and, further, the cycleshed adds additional valences. Hop on a bike for any reasonable amount of time and one's sense of time transforms: The rhythmic revolutions of riding any kind of cycle can be meditative, in a word. The simple repetition of the turning of cranks provides a movement that enables what some describe as a "flow state," and the energy expended offers a platform for mindful breathing practices. Moving at a speed that is sensible to humans without overwhelming the senses, the bicycle and its various offshoots enable the agency and autonomy that is offered by other, more modern forms of transportation technology without the emissions that often accompany them, never mind the classist barriers that gatekeep them.

A few quick caveats:

The cycleshed could certainly be read as ableist—the cycleshed expanding and contracting on account of ability. But the adaptability of the cycle for those of varying abilities, now coupled with the surge of affordable electric cycles, may actually lend itself to equity more than one would think. Yes, some could travel farther than others. But to fixate on this is to miss the point: the cycleshed is about the creation of communities in which all have equitable access to that which they need at a reasonable distance. The cycleshed incites the aspirational reorientation of our perspectives in order to bring about communities in which all—regardless of ability—have what they need to *flourish*. And improved cycling infrastructure would benefit the safety of those using mobility devices such as wheelchairs in addition to the cyclists. The cycleshed is not about how far an individual can travel as much as what can be made possible within reasonable bounds for a community through democratic discernment, infrastructure investment, and the like.

The cycleshed could also be interpreted as Luddite—a proposal advocating a return to preindustrial technologies and the meaningful advances they've offered in some areas of life such as medicine. Rather, the cycleshed is an embrace of purposeful technology that benefits Earth and its inhabitants. More than anything, it's a solarpunk[16] vision of communities that are no longer overrun by multinational corporations but instead populated by local efforts to make life meaningful and good by working within and drawing from their contexts.

And, lastly, the cycleshed could be understood as regressive, harkening to a time in which one's kin lived in the same village, if not the same abode. My family lives on both coasts of the United States, and I in its forgotten center. It may sound like living closely to one's bikeshed is a prescriptive luxury, asking us to forsake those beyond it. Hardly. Or that's far from my intention anyway. There's no purity that's possible in this world. We inherit the impurities, pollutants, and errors of the past.[17] Still, it's worth imagining better ways—regardless of, perhaps even *because of,* their imperfection. Could we live 50 percent of our lives—that is, all that we consume, wear, build, dispose, imbibe, or create—within the cycleshed? Eighty percent? More? And for the aspects of our lives that might lie beyond this region, reinvigorated high-speed railway systems could connect cyclesheds.[18]

The cycleshed could be viewed in any number of ways. But, at its core, this concept—as inspiration and aspiration—simply asks of us the following:

What does it mean to be gathered in community? And how far does community, as such, extend? What is the scope of our care? What is a sensible scale of love? What if we allowed the bicycle to transform our sense of scale and thus our commitment to place?

With the urgencies of global climate change amplifying daily, there may be a temptation to spread oneself thin, to give oneself over to overcaring, to be everything to everyone. The revolution of the cycle suggests a commitment to the local that is also a faithfulness to the planetary.

The world cannot be saved. The cycle teaches us that there's no such thing as the world, only countless places woven indiscreetly. By caring for *places*, we might be able to practice regenerative relationships with the planet.

But perhaps this revolution is a pipe dream long gone.

൙

Remediation

On warm afternoons—of which there are plenty these days—my partner and I often go for a casual ride on the path not far from our home. Multiuse paths are far from novel in many places. But, in our midwestern city, there are only approximately four within a fifteen-mile radius, and that's only if you choose to count meager stretches of performatively protected bike lanes.

This path—at least for us—is a rare treat: respite from internal combustion and the risky boxes of steel that it powers. We see couples strolling, dogs sniffing shrubs, university students carrying groceries, children zipping around on scooters, squirrels darting with acorns aplenty. It's one of the few places left with no expectation of spending money or being "productive."

There's no such thing as loitering in a commons. It's called resting. Chatting. Communing. Being. Call it *life*.

Zinnia blossoms line intersections with patchworks of color, and milkweed stands tall, proud home for monarchs and pantry for bees. There's invasive honeysuckle, too, though. Plenty of it.

It's not perfect. But a path like this does seem to *remediate* our polluted communities long choked out by semitruck emissions, segregated by redlining, disenfranchised by gerrymandering, brutalized by overpolicing, poisoned by food deserts.

It's a vision of what *could be* in the presently car-dominated landscape of the United States.

Roads turned to pathways. Highways to walkways.

"Swords into plowshares."

⚘

A Meditation on Pain

My father is an exceptional athlete. For my entire life, this has always been the case.

He's one of those people who is naturally quite good at most any challenge he throws himself at, and he can do it on a diet of fried eggs and sour candy or whatever else. He has competed in countless races across multiple disciplines of sport—running, swimming, climbing, mountaineering, paddling, and of course cycling.

My father's most recent competitive streak has taken him into the ungodly world of Ironman triathlons: a 2.4-mile swim, a 112-mile bike, followed by a marathon 26.2-mile run. Don't ask me why. I couldn't tell you.

My sister now has kids of her own, doing her best to pass along the very best of our parents to her little ones, my dear niblings. On a recent visit to my sister's home, my dad and I caught a glimpse of this as my sister soothed her youngest, feverishly resisting a nap, with a tune I hadn't heard in years.

She sang:

> I see the moon
> The moon sees me
> The moon sees somebody I want to see.
> God bless the moon
>
> And God bless me
> And God bless somebody I want to see.

Memories tumbled forth, reliving moments I'd long forgotten, unlocked now by this jingle: a tune sung to me since before I could remember, which nurtured me through my parents' divorce and the trying years that followed. But this reminiscing was interrupted:

"I sing that, you know," my dad said.

"Huh?"

"I sing that when I really hurt," he continued.

"Wait, what?"

"You know, like, when I'm in the middle of a race—like during the bike portion of an Ironman—and I really hurt bad, I sing that."

It didn't make much sense, but I couldn't shake the thought. An elite athlete, when at the height of physical toil and at the very limits of what his body can accomplish, sings a nursery rhyme once sung to him by his own mother?

There's this thing that some cyclists and runners and others call the "pain cave." It's the very depths of physical and mental fatigue, the place you go when everything in your body is screaming for you to quit. When everything in you wants to give up and you begin the mental dialogue of "questioning it all," *that's* the pain cave. As runner Sam Robinson describes it, "The pain cave is a place where we take stock of our courage and ask ourselves how much we are willing to give for the goals we've laid out."[19] It's a bewildering and exhilarating and isolating experience. Those of us who encounter this—whether by choice or by force, whether in athletics or some other facet of life—each deal with it differently. My father chooses to sing a nursery rhyme.

I got curious, knowing that this sweet tune must have had a history beyond my pianist grandmother.

The earliest record of it that I could find is the 1784 nursery rhyme collection (with a subtitle so epic that it couldn't be omitted here), *Gammer Gurton's Garland, or, The Nursery Parnassus: A Choice Collection of Pretty Songs and Verses for the Amusement of All Little Good Children Who Can Neither Read nor Run,* which includes the core of the song: "I see the moon, and the moon sees me / God bless the moon, and God bless me."[20]

The addition of the portion "The moon sees somebody I want to see" came about sometime thereafter, recorded in the 1896 book by Clifton Johnson, *What They Say in New England: A Book of Signs, Sayings, and Superstition.*[21] In it, Johnson writes this descriptor of the tune:

> Look at the moon some night and say,—
> "I see the moon, the moon sees me; The moon sees somebody I want to see."
> Then name the person you wish to see, and in a day or two you will see that person.[22]

Curiously, at some point prior to 1896, this nursery rhyme took on a mystic flair—a way of *communing* with those afar but soon-to-be-near.

A 2012 psychological study demonstrated the role of music in elevating both pain threshold and positive affect.[23] Interestingly, however, it was not music "in general" that did this; passive listening to music didn't produce endorphins or other contributing factors to the elevation of pain threshold or positive affect. Rather, it was the *active production* of music that led to these results, the actual *act* of singing and drumming and the like. This correlation seems to explain the social bonding capacities of music and dance that have long been identified by anthropologists and sociologists, among others.[24]

At the limits of physical exhaustion, my father does what humans have always done: gathered with others—present, ancestral, and beyond—in pain and in solidarity. He sings a silly tune that brings him face to face with his late mother, his children, and now his grandchildren—and perhaps those who come after.

I'd like to think that my father sings because he knows he's not alone—and thus perhaps relieved—even in suffering.

Cycling isn't always easy. And if each chapter of this book has ended with some sort of practice to take on—some instruction of how to incarnate these parables—I encourage you with this simple suggestion:

If you find yourself on a bike ride, huffing up a hill, legs on fire and heavy as lead, when all you can think to do is give up . . .

If you find yourself exhausted by fossil-fuel corporations' ecocidal destruction . . .

Or overwhelmed with an economy that leaves millions destitute . . .

Or painfully yearning to realize a community accessible by cycle . . . ?

Sing.

Sing *in defiance.*

Sing *in communion.*

Repairing

Greasy Joy

"I'm having fun. I'm having fun. I'm having fun," I mutter to myself with excessive breath.

This is how I convince myself that I'm, somehow, well, having fun after I've stripped a bolt or broken a spoke or smashed my knuckles into the cement because a wrench slipped. Usually after a few initial expletives.

I fix up old bikes "for fun." That's what I say anyway.

Really, I do it because it's something that I find meaningful. It adds a tactile dimension to my life that's excessively digital, driven by endless emails and online learning management systems and all that. It's greasy and rusty and dirty and often quite difficult. But it's good.

And this is because manual labor rewards in ways that intellectual labor never could.

Of course, the distinction between these two forms of labor is a farce. This bifurcation of labor diminishes the critical intellect needed for manual labor. That this is how labor is generally categorized is telling. The intellect needed to tailor or cobble or cook or fix is immense. "Unskilled labor" is a capitalist lie. As someone who has done both full-time, I feel confident in saying that getting a PhD doesn't require any more intellect than farming. Both demand intellect. Different forms of intellect, sure: Each requires different patterns of thought, skill sets, practices, rituals, and the like. But creating a hierarchy of valuation is a joke. Diminishing the work of those who feed and clothe and house and hydrate and transport with care is foolish.

I, like many others, enjoy seeing the results of my toil. The outcomes of my efforts are direct and evident. It is immediately rewarding without being tantamount to cheap instant gratification. Repairing bikes is how I try to make myself useful beyond the classroom, giving life to rusted machines and gifting movement to friends and strangers alike.

I can't begin to tell you how many times, in the process of fixing one part, I've broken another. It used to be the case that I could almost always count on creating an additional problem in my effort to fix some other. One step forward, two steps back.

This happens less now. It still happens—just far less frequently. This is partially due to more experience and actually having the correct tools for the job. But it's *mostly* due to the fact that I work much more slowly now. Or, more accurately, I spend much more time *noticing* the cycle and *gathering* information.

I've realized that most of the process of repairing—at least on the old, beat-up bikes that I work on—takes place as I encounter and develop a relationship with the thing. Pausing. Listening. Assuming a different angle, indeed, *perspective*. Observing. Making notes.

Most of the process of repair happens far before a wrench ever touches the bike.

Slowing down actually makes the work happen far more quickly, or at least effectively, as fewer additional complications arise. Of course, unanticipatable things still happen, even when I've approached a repair mindfully. A bolt seizes. A cable frays. Even the most care-full mechanics encounter troubles they didn't see coming.

But *repairing* is nothing without *noticing* or *gathering*. Without pause, without relationship, repair will almost always create additional harm. Only in slowing and communing can real restoration take place.

Dirty. Grimy. Greasy. And overjoyed.

∽

The need for repair—of communities, of politics, of bioregions—is immense.

But rushing too quickly to repair often leads to us overlooking one thing or another. Jumping to conclusions—let alone "solutions"—rarely works out, at least in my experience. You know the deal: "When you assume . . ." For this reason, this book has invited you to spend considerable time pausing, slowing, noticing, collecting, gathering. In so doing, we are better able to attend to—indeed tend to—the crises of climate catastrophe. Meaningful repair is predicated on noticing problems—and their causes—in addition to possibilities for response. These processes enable us to better repair our common home.

Yes, the severity of our planet's precarity demands meaningful repair *now*. *Already*. And this has been true since at least the 1970s, when ExxonMobil predicted climate crisis, buried the data, and then persisted with their exploitation of the environment *knowingly*.[1] And, certainly, the lack of any sort of meaningful, comprehensive response to climate change since NASA scientist James Hansen's report to Congress in 1988 is utterly inexcusable. When my students learn of this history, they are horrified yet also liberated from their guilt that they are somehow the "cause" of climate change. They're complicit, to be sure. But they've inherited their complicity.

Still, to act with *urgency* is not the same as to act with *haste*. Urgent repair is needed; hasty repair will only cause further damage.

Quick fixes rarely aid in long-term flourishing. For this reason, the geo-engineering plans that are currently proposed, such as atmospheric aerosol sprays, should be viewed with great suspicion—especially if these solutions are tied in any way to any one individual's or corporation's own profit.

We must think differently about our approach to climate repair.

Imagine a pipe bursts in your basement, causing quite a flood. Do you run to grab a bucket to start bailing water? No! Not if you've any sense at least. What do you do? You shut off the water, of course. You cut off the problem at its source. You first determine the cause and stop it (i.e., turning off the burst pipe) before attending to the effects (i.e., the flood).

Meaningful repair seeks to mend the root cause of the problem and not merely the symptoms thereof.

Immediately bailing water without addressing the cause exhibits good but ultimately misplaced effort. At best, it's a stopgap measure. But if we're being honest, in the long term, it's futile work.

The difference between repairing symptomatic effects versus repairing root causes is precisely the difference between *charity* and *justice*.

Charity helps a bit now but rarely cuts off the problem at the source. It feeds the hungry now—which is *good*, of course—but doesn't question why people are going hungry in the first place. It gives temporary shelter to those experiencing homelessness—which is *good*, of course—but doesn't address an economic system that allows private-equity firms to take over an entire housing market, never mind a political system that refuses to acknowledge health care as a basic human right, thus leaving its people to languish from addiction, mental illness, and more. Charity is good but ultimately insufficient.

Trying to fix, say, post-incarceration recidivism rates in the United States without addressing atrocious incarceration practices is insufficient, just as trying to end mass incarceration without tackling matters like unemployment rates, food deserts, public school funding, minimum sentencing laws, peremptory juror challenges, public housing, health-care accessibility, and the like is inadequate. Or to subject people to a crushing economic system with unlivable wages, a housing market dominated by hedge fund–backed real estate firms, a classist health-care system with few resources for mental illness, and then to criminalize those same people when they end up experiencing homelessness—*individualizing* a problem that is *social* and *systemic* through and through—is sinful.

The repair that I'm interested in is the work of *justice*: fixing problems at their root. Hence the need to slow, notice, and gather prior to repair. When effects overwhelm, identifying causes demands mindful attention.

The act of making hope is not only accomplished in repair. Hope-making is the entire process of noticing, gathering, *and* repairing. Each requires the other in a reciprocal and heterarchical way.

∽

Making Change

Processes of change-making are not neat or tidy or clean. They're odd and slant and messy.

The final section of this book centers on opportunities for change-making, emphasizing practices of *tikkun olam*—the Kabbalist term referring to the practice of world-mending. These concluding chapters aim to illustrate practices of change-making that can function as reparative models for justice-seeking movements.

Repair must move at the speed of urgency, witnessing to a vision of another possible world—regenerative, relational, resurrective.

But repair is not final, is not finished. It's provisional. It's processual. Something's bound to go awry eventually. And so, we mend.

Sowing

Tiny Prayers

Every time, it's the same. I never have faith. Or if I do, it's no bigger than the seed in my palm.

"Lord, I believe. Help my unbelief."

You'd think that it would get easier. Every time, I tell myself that it'll feel better—more certain—than I remember it. It doesn't. Or it hasn't for me anyway. I'm starting to think that it won't.

"Help my unbelief."

Fingertips plunge into soil to bury possibility itself. Fingers scrape dirt to cover the divot. Palms press the earth, and the earth, always, presses back. As ecophilosopher David Abram writes, "Although we've lately come to associate gravity with heaviness, and so to think of it as having a strictly downward vector, nonetheless *something rises up into us* from the solid earth whenever we're in contact with it."[1] We're met in this—in every—encounter.

There, in that muddy matrix, is this kernel held—as am I.

"Help my unbelief."

My knees rest on the soil. The tops of my feet ache. This prayerful posture takes its toll on my body. And I lament that my hope for future flourishing is hardly yet the size of a mustard seed, even on my best days.

But what else is there to do? Give up? Sure. That'll help. My neighbors' kids who love to run across the street for a ripe heirloom tomato—the taste of summer—wouldn't appreciate my apathy.

If certainty is what I'm after, then I suppose I better quit sowing seeds. Nothing would be more certain than the not-growing that not-sowing would accomplish. Certainty achieved.

Another handful makes it way from pocketed packet to palm. Seeds scatter. Sprinkled prayers shower earth.

"Help my unbelief."

∽

Sowing, Simply

What can one say about sowing that doesn't come across as pedantic? As patronizing?

I'll spare you the description. You know what sowing is: Seed. Dirt. Seed in dirt.

Yeah, it can be complex, considering adequate depth, interval, row spacing, timing, and so on. And sowing leads to questions regarding companion planting, crop rotation, nutrient availability, critter mitigation (or, in more conventional terms, "pest control"), and so on.

But you know what it is: seed in dirt.

∽

The Courage to Sow

Climate science is pretty clear at this point: there is no winning. Things will not get better. Not even close. At best, there is only minimizing losses. There's no stopping, no turning around, no reversing climate change at this stage. It's too late.

This is not hopelessness. I don't think that it's nihilism, either. It's realism, because this is our current reality as suggested by every recent report from the Intergovernmental Panel on Climate Change.[2]

"Climate change" is an inadequate term now. "Climate catastrophe" is far closer to what's already here and still yet impending.

In the now-famous words of journalist David Wallace-Wells, "It is worse, much worse, than you think."[3]

You might be asking yourself, *Wait. Isn't this supposed to be a book about hope?*

Indeed! But hope is not optimism—the unfounded belief that things will get better regardless of whether I am or others are doing anything about them—nor is it synonymous with certain success—the guarantee that one's desired outcomes will, in fact, occur.

Truth be told, both optimism and pessimism are utterly *certain.* It *will* work out. It *won't* work out. And if either is guaranteed, then my actions mean naught. It'll be what it'll be—irrespective of my responsibility or lack thereof. Oddly enough, it might then be the case that both optimism and pessimism actually function as expressions of nihilism: sheer certainty about the future such that apathy is the *only* possible response thereto.

But, as Jenny Odell reminds, "Neither our lives nor the life of the planet is a foregone conclusion."[4] And this is because each now-moment is shot through with *uncertainty.* Each instant is the pulsing of indeterminacy, which, thus, enables creativity. Odell contends that at the "fundamental uncertainty that lives at the heart of every single moment" is "where our agency also lives."[5] Because of the uncertainty seeded in each moment, our future need not be ceded to indifference, inaction, or desolation.

Hope could yet be, as philosopher Hannah Arendt proposes, the indeterminate potential that the "smallest act in the most limited circumstances bears the seed of the same boundlessness, because one deed, and sometimes one word, suffices to change every constellation."[6] No guarantees. Zero assurances. Solely *potentiality.*

Hope is founded on *uncertainty.* Uncertainty is the necessary precondition for hope. Why else would a thing like hope be needed if it weren't always in response to uncertain and precarious conditions? The indeterminacy at the heart of each moment is the very ground of hope. Uncertainty is the soil that holds the kernels of our prayerful actions.

Because it is founded on uncertainty, nothing could be more fallacious than to suggest that hope is synonymous with success. We make a mockery of hope when we equate it with a surefire outcome.

If hope is not synonymous with success, then what is hope anyway? Hope is sowing: a necessary action without surety—"that which will have had to happen."[7]

Or, in a word, *faith*.

Today, it seems that the term "faith" has been watered down entirely. Or, rather, it's been misconstrued. But what if we practiced opening ourselves to the possibility of alternative conceptions of this fraught term?

Typically, "faith" is considered synonymous with a belief in a particular truth-claim. Often, "belief" is associated with rational knowledge of some sort: "to believe" is an extension of "to know." By associating belief and rational knowledge, we erode the work of theology—traditionally defined as "faith seeking understanding." Notice that faith and ways of knowing are related but not identical. Faith is not "what" one knows, nor is simply "how" one knows, which would make it synonymous with mere "belief." That one believes something to be true does not, *with necessity*, make it true. But many think that truth stems from belief: hence, the prevalence of climate denialism, election denialism, COVID-19 denialism, vaccination denialism, and so forth. Believability does not determine veracity, *especially* if one's beliefs are indistinguishable from self-serving confirmation bias. How might we rethink faith and, thus, hope?

As process theologian Catherine Keller reminds us, if the work of theology is "faith *seeking* understanding," then those who wish to think theologically cannot comfort themselves with "faith that already understands and so no longer needs to seek." Keller continues, "Theology is not itself the faith but its quest. If we stop seeking, we are no longer *on the way*. Faith seeking understanding has . . . turned into 'belief that understands.'"[8]

If by faith we mean some kind of "propositional knowledge,"

then we have lost our way. To arrest "faith" and coerce it to fit within neat dogmatic boxes that are intelligible to us makes an idol out of the ultimate. Faith as "knowledge" turns it into something one *has* as opposed to *does*. It becomes an object of possession to be wielded as one pleases; and, if faith is to be "had" through "knowing," then one's relationship to that object of knowledge ceases as soon as one has it—static, frozen, perhaps even dead.

Surely, even the divinity we try to convey eludes our limited categories, finite language, and partial perspectives in its infinitude. Even our *names* for divinity are wholly inadequate, and the Hebrew Bible reminds us of this when God introduces Godself to Moses at the burning bush (Exodus) not with a traditional noun but an oddly verbal phrase: "I am who I am." From this account, it seems that nouns may even be too static for the ultimate.

All I'm trying to say is that we must approach any such truth-claim—especially about matters so vital—with a bit of humility. I mean, isn't it a bit presumptive—maybe even a bit arrogant—to assume that we can know the divine in its totality and eternality? This is true even of our closest human companions like longtime friends, family members, and partners, whom we know with deep intimacy yet are never really fully known to us: they continue to surprise us! Thus, every such attempt to articulate "the truth" is at best incomplete.

So, what if faith wasn't about *merely* knowing or believing? What if it was even more holistic? What if we maintained the inherent connection between faith and *faithfulness*—verbal, fleshy, incarnate?

What if, as an alternative, we considered faith as "the state of being *ultimately concerned,*" as existentialist theologian Paul Tillich puts it? Tillich explains,

> Man [*sic*], like every living being, is concerned about many things, above all about those which condition his very existence, such as food and shelter. But man . . . has spiritual

concerns—cognitive, aesthetic, social, political. Some of them are urgent, often extremely urgent, and each of them as well as the vital concerns can claim ultimacy for a human life or the life of a social group. If it claims ultimacy it demands the total surrender of him who accepts this claim, and it promises total fulfillment even if all other claims have to be subjected to it or rejected in its name.[9]

Essentially, Tillich asks us: What is it that you orient your life around? What is your life dedicated to? What do you worship—not in your "beliefs" so much as your day-in, day-out, lived reality? We all worship something, regardless of our religious identity. We all orient our lives around something that becomes elevated to the status of ultimacy. What is that for you? For me?

Faith could thus be conceptualized as the dynamics of that which ultimately concerns us—the ways in which the inexpressible longing that consumes our whole being orients us in each moment. This may be conscious or unconscious. Oof. And it may have been an active choice or a passive acceptance. Yikes. And, still yet worse, regardless of whether we've actively chosen it, it's possible that it could be *misplaced,* even if it's "good." All kinds of good things might concern us but lack the capacity to fulfill us at the level of ultimacy: for example, being a good parent, a caring spouse, an effective teacher, a skilled farmer, a helping carpenter. These things are good but become idols if they subsume us as our ultimate concern. This is what Tillich refers to as the "risk of faith," "for if it proves to be a failure, the meaning of one's life breaks down."[10] Faith, thus, describes the relationship between our selves and our total commitment to that which concerns us ultimately.

How might all this theological pondering relate to sowing?

First, faith, in this view, becomes something so much more than a compartmentalized and separable set of doctrines, dogmas, or creeds that one either knows or doesn't know. This view makes faith the very ground of our lifeways, becoming much more robust than just what we believe. Faith as ultimate concern deconstructs the assumption of faith as purely intellectualistic or utterly emotional, instead functioning as *existential*, which is also to say *contextual* and *bioregional*. Faith thus grounds our being and is not a mere component thereof. This means that faith cannot—indeed, must not—be divorced from matters of fact, rationality, and the like. There need not be any tension between "faith" and "reason" nor "religion" and "science" in this sketch.

Put differently: Because, as Tillich writes, "faith is a total and centered act of the personal self, the act of unconditional, infinite, and ultimate concern," then faith must be and can only be *holistic:* grounded in thought, emotion, embodiment, ecology, history.[11] It cannot be abstracted from time, nor can it be extracted from place. Faith emerges at the confluence of our becoming in the world in each moment.

Second, because faith is *existential* through and through, then faith need not be considered separate from, much less opposite to, *doubt*. On this point, Tillich argues, "If faith is understood as belief that something is true, doubt is incompatible with the act of faith. If faith is understood as being ultimately concerned, *doubt is a necessary element in it.* It is a consequence of the risk of faith."[12] That one doubts need not mean that one has failed at being faithful: "Existential doubt and faith are poles of the same reality, the state of ultimate concern," and, thus, "serious doubt is the confirmation of faith. It indicates the seriousness of the concern, its unconditional character."[13] If, by faith, we mean the *risking of everything* on that which one has deemed ultimate, then doubt is a necessary element therein, which only makes sense given that we're talking about the ultimate risk that one can run.

Faith and doubt are entangled. Hence, the proclamation "Lord, I believe. Help my unbelief" may not be an oxymoron at all.

Third, and finally, because faith and doubt are interconnected, this is why Tillich contends that faith is fundamentally enacted as an expression of courage: "One cannot replace faith by courage, but neither can one describe faith without courage."[14] It's worth quoting him at length:

> Doubt is overcome not by repression but by courage. Courage does not deny that there is doubt, but it takes the doubt into itself as an expression of its own finitude and affirms the content of an ultimate concern. Courage does not need the safety of an unquestionable conviction. It includes the risk without which no creative life is possible.[15]

If faith cannot be considered unswerving certainty but is always predicated on precarious uncertainty, then "courage as an element of faith is the daring self-affirmation of one's own being in spite of the powers of 'nonbeing.'" Hence, "ultimate concern is ultimate risk and ultimate courage."[16] Elsewhere, Tillich suggests that courage is "the act of the individual self in taking the anxiety of nonbeing upon itself by affirming itself as either part of an embracing whole or in its individual selfhood."[17] Courage allows us to simultaneously embrace our individual agency as well as our interconnectedness with our ecologies in spite of threats of nonbeing.

This whole analysis, however compelling, has been an attempt to lead us to these two key questions:

- What could be a riskier, indeed more menacingly powerful, force of nonbeing than global climate catastrophe?
- What does a meaningful response to the unthinkable destruction caused by climate change look like when one knows that saving the planet is no longer possible?

Faithfulness as solely "knowing" the "right stuff" seems inadequate for making sense of, much less responding to, our planetary crisis. We need something far more existential, and thus contextual and bioregional. We need a conception of hope—and thus hopeful praxis—that contends with the scope and scale of this crisis, all the while acknowledging the impossibility of responding adequately at this scope and scale.

Hope is the courageous "in spite of"—uncertain but not timid, doubting but not apathetic.

Hope is the courage to sow.

ॐ

On Doing the Right Thing

Why try to do the right thing?

In a recorded lecture, ethicist Miguel De La Torre asks the audience, "When there is no hope of winning, do you still struggle for justice? Do you struggle for justice because you expect an award at the end of the battle?" He presses them further, "Do you do justice because you know you're going to win? Or do you do justice *for the sake of justice?*"

When there is no hope of winning, why try? When victory is impossible, why not just give up and save your energy?

I, like De La Torre, submit to you something entirely different:

Faithfulness is not about winning. It's not about success. Maybe those things occur, but likely not. Frankly, it seems like they won't when it comes to global climate catastrophe.

So, why do anything at all? Why sow? What good is it anyway?

All I can hear is De La Torre, echoing, "When there is no hope of winning, do you still struggle for justice?"

De La Torre responds to his own questions in his lecture: "I do [justice] because *it defines my humanity.*" He continues, "My praxis, my actions, defines who I am as a human being, and it defines who I am as a Christian. . . . It defines our very humanity."

The enactment of *justice itself* matters—irrespective of its success or failure. De La Torre thus invites us to *embrace hopelessness* for the sake of hopeful faithfulness. When there is no hope of winning, we must still strive for justice for the sake of justice because it defines our humanity.

Hopeful praxis—the *practice itself* and *not* whether that practice has led to some great victory—defines our very humanity.

Thus, the hopelessness that emerges when victory is not possible is *the very catalyst for hopeful praxis.* The faithfulness that is practiced "in spite of" defines the very nature of hope. Hope is the embodiment of the *nevertheless.* Like faith and doubt, hopelessness and hope are intertwined: the latter exists precisely because of the former. As womanist theologians like Monica A. Coleman have put it, hope is "making a way out of no way."[18] But a way is not an end, nor is that way necessarily gilded with perfection. It is just that: a way where there has been a wall.

Whether the seeds I sow sprout forth matters not. Of course, I strive to tend to and abide with them to every extent possible, working to create conditions that might allow growth. I weed and mulch and trellis and water for the sake of possible growth. But I cannot create, indeed cannot *force,* this growth. I must simply strive to make a way for growth.

Mengzi, the Confucian philosopher, once offered a parable about the "man from Song." This man from Song was so worried about the condition of the grain he had planted that he attempted to "help the grain grow" by pulling on it. In this ignorant process, the man from Song only achieved the withering of his crops. The moral of this tale? Mengzi reasons, "One must work at [righteousness], but do not aim at it directly. Let the heart not forget, but do not help it grow" (*Mengzi* 2A2).

Through sowing, we learn that hope is incarnating a world that is not yet but *must be.* But, as with the man from Song, hope cannot force the materialization of that longed-for world. Hope is sowing, tending, abiding—and no more. No certainty dwells here.

Hope, thus, is not salvific. It does not save, because it cannot guarantee this. It's not about success or salvation so much as witnessing to *salvific possibility,* which cannot come from us. We can only embrace hope's invitation and inhabit the faithful praxis by creating conditions in which resurrection might be possible.

Here we can begin to meditate on one final mystery that Tillich shares with us: "Every act of faith presupposes participation in that toward which it is directed."[19] If it is true to say that every act of faith points toward our ultimate concern—that which grounds our being—then it is also true to say that every act of faith "participates in that to which it points."[20] Therefore, when we enact justice for the least of these, we participate in the merciful love that makes justice possible. When we sow, we take part in the unthinkable creativity from which life emerges. An act of faith is the ushering in of the kindom of God. In a holy act of faith, we become entangled with the mystery of love—the seed that sprouts at the heart of it all.

⅋

Seeding Faith

In Mark's Gospel, we get this interesting moment: Jesus, attempting to describe the beloved community he likes to refer to as the kingdom of God, muses,

> With what can we compare the kingdom of God, or what parable will we use for it? It is like a mustard seed, which, when sown upon the ground, is the smallest of all the seeds on earth, yet when it is sown it grows up and becomes the greatest of all shrubs and puts forth large branches, so that the birds of the air can make nests in its shade. (Mark 4:30–32)

Growing up, I always assumed that this brief parable was about how only a small amount of faith—which I took to mean "belief"—was needed and would grow into something much larger. If I believed just enough, I would soon really, truly, actually believe and, thus, reap the rewards. I just needed to get the ball rolling, so to speak. But, funny enough, the parable isn't about the mustard seed nor what it grows into. Not really. Or at least not entirely.

Jesus seems to suggest that the kingdom of God is like this tiny, impossible, unlikely thing that, with nurture and care, can become a space of respite, relief, and belonging.

It's not about the seed or shrub. It's about what the mustard seed-shrub makes possible. The parable is not about what it becomes as much as what it enables: hospitality, gathering, refuge. Yes, the mustard seed-shrub must grow large enough to do so, but the point isn't that it becomes large in and of and for itself! A big shrub. Big deal. What's emphasized here is not the growth spurt so much as how its growth precipitates further creative advance: it extends the webs of interconnection by which our cosmos is constituted. Mustard seeds multiply possibility, just as love begets love.

Seeds do not grow because they "know" they're going to "win"—but because growth and flourishing, in the right context and under just circumstances, are good. The multiplication of respite, belonging, and generosity offered by the mustard seed-shrub is not guaranteed, but its sowing is "that which will have had to happen" for that goodness to be made possible.

Unfortunately, global climate change threatens to upend everything. And it does so by rupturing the webs that compose our food chains, ocean conveyor belts, jet streams, and so on.

Do I think we—particularly those of us who bear disproportionate responsibility for our society's carbon emissions, nuclear contamination, oceanic dead zones, and the like—should do everything in our power to prevent as much damage to our planet as we possibly can? Absolutely. No question.

Do I think we should act accordingly *because* we're going to be successful? Not at all. We can't know that, and pretending like this is even likely would be a lie. As Trappist monk Thomas Merton recommended,

> Do not depend on the hope of the results. . . . You may have to face the fact that your work will be apparently worthless and even achieve no result at all, if not perhaps results op-

posite to what you expect. As you get used to this idea you start more and more to concentrate not on the results but on the value, the rightness, the truth of the work itself.[21]

And why does Merton think this? "The real hope, then, is not in something we think we can do, but in God who is making something good out of it in some way we cannot see."[22] Mustard seeds must be sown, but we cannot "grow" them ourselves. As the great Rabbi Tarfon taught, "It is not incumbent on you to complete the work [of perfecting the world]. But you are not free to evade it."[23]

The cards are stacked against us.

Yet what else is there to do but sow?

☙

A Practice to Practice Sowing

❧

Lawns are practically useless. They're the remnant of bourgeois nobility flaunting their wealth, showing off that they hadn't the need to cultivate their land for subsistence farming but could instead use it for ornamental "beauty" in the form of nonnative grasses.

Of course, grasses can provide crucial spaces for recreation, becoming all the more important as public infrastructure such as parks continue to see divestment in nation-states like the United States. And recognizing the inequitable access that Black and Brown communities have to public green spaces makes some of these grass-covered spaces crucial. But many lawns do not serve this vital role.

To this end, some studies have suggested that turf grasses are now "the single largest irrigated crop" in the United States.[24] And yet we continue to fill what little space has not been covered by concrete with these same grasses. In the face of amplified droughts, food shortages, and insect collapse, there are far better uses available.

Should you have a lawn you care for, consider the benefits of replacing this lawn—or even just some portion of it—with perennial wildflowers for pollinators or a vegetable garden. Removing the grass is relatively easy: cover the lawn with a tarp of some kind (weighing it down sufficiently so it doesn't take flight and sail to some distant land) for a few weeks to kill the grass; then it can be removed in chunks with just a spade, cutting squares out just below the roots. There are even easier methods like using a sod cutter; this specialized tool makes the work easier, but it's far from necessary. The bare soil can be supplemented with compost or additional topsoil, but that's also not absolutely crucial and will simply depend on your soil. Regional wildflower mixes can be found for any bioregion, and vegetables suited for your area can be found via any growing zone map.

Will these efforts—in isolation—solve climate change? Nope. Will they bring respite to pollinators and hospitality to neighbors—human and more-than-human alike—for whatever "time that remains"? Surely.

What we might consider hopeless is certainly not meaningless.

By sowing, we witness to a world imagined otherwise, which is to say more diverse and, thus, bountiful.

May it be so.

Mending

The Task of Mending

It's early afternoon on a summery Sunday—one of those days that I've somehow, mostly unintentionally, managed to keep from busying myself too much.

Annoyed, I remember the various clothes with various holes forming a small pile in my closet. I've been trying to put them out of my mind, aware of the time and attention that they'll need. I think especially of the few wool socks that I've waited just a bit too long to retire to this pile, fearing that they have surpassed the threshold for darn-ability. Surely, there's something else I can do this afternoon?

Nevertheless, the holey clothes call to me, and I'm left with no choice but to rummage for a slightly bent needle and a bit of thread that's close in color but I know won't match. So it goes.

As I sift through the pile, sorting out which garment I'll work on first, memories seem to topple one over the next. A piece of glass snags my supposedly reinforced jeans while cleaning out a creek bed in rural West Virginia. A button from a beloved flannel jacket flies across my damp basement floor, apparently displeased about the recent rinse cycle. The rough texture of Shawangunk Conglomerate cheese-grates the shoulder of a sun shirt midway through a rock-climbing route.

This fabric holds stories my body seems to have forgotten.

I watch these memories pass by and wonder. These worn and

worn-out clothes each tell a story—often a story of some sort of less-than-ideal moment. Something went awry. Something didn't go quite as planned. The pile grows.

So, my needle plunges into the fabric—and occasionally my fingertip, because the clumsiness that led to these holes also applies to my sewing skills. I'm still learning to mend in the ways that my forebears did. But I also know that I'll always continue learning to mend, as each garment—each hole, each story—demands my careful attention to its contours, weight, draping, and so on. Even similar mends are never exactly the same. I know that each tear and each patch are unique, requiring that I stay as present as possible to the passing of needle and thread—stitching together the past and present.

Sometimes my mind wanders while mending, and it's usually not long thereafter that I realize that I had the fabric stretched the wrong way or I accidentally tacked both sides of the fabric together or something like that. I fix the error and continue on—and sometimes I just have to start over—nevertheless satisfied with the improvements that soon will gift new life to this object: this cloth that will become a small home to my body.

As I near the end of this work, I realize that I've not left myself enough thread. Typical. The finishing knot will inevitably be makeshift because of this oversight, but it'll do. It almost always does.

◌⁑

Visible Mending

Mending refers to the process of repairing textiles, usually by patching, darning, or the like. "*Visible* mending," as it's come to be known of late,[1] refers to intentionally maintaining the visibility of the repair, once complete. In other words, counter to other clothing alteration practices (e.g., tailoring), visible mending not only avoids hiding or obfuscating the repair but actually highlights and draws attention to the repair.

By using mismatching thread, contrasting colors, even clashing patterns, visible mending declines to hide so-called "flaws"; instead, it uses "damage" as a site for the creation of more than mere repair—the creation of beauty. Visible mending marries the pursuit of longevity with the genesis of aesthetic delight.

Visible mending is a strange thing: equal parts art and utility, just as much about creativity as it is function. Thread and fabric work in concert in an effort to render brokenness usable again. But it renders that "brokenness" *visible* even as it toils to repair. Stitches catch our eye; patches contrast their canvas, if only minorly. These things make us actually notice—and sometimes even *want* to notice—the history of that garment. We're confronted by it, in fact.

Repair—using the tools, resources, and capacities accessible to the mender—is the priority; the focus is on ongoing relation and persistent flourishing. But visible mending does so without pretending that the garment's past has been without damage. The history of that which is mended nearly always remains evident, if not obvious. This practice of mending seeks not the feigned beauty of perfection so much as the eye-catching intrigue of patchworks.

As a contrast to the extraordinary expertise necessary to *invisibly* stitch, patch, or even construct a garment, visible mending is an *accessible* practice requiring few tools and minimal skills. I assure you: if I can mend, so, too, can you.

The values of sustainability, frugality, simplicity, resourcefulness, and the like are hard to miss in a practice like mending. Mending rebuts the harmful currents of consumerism, fast fashion, and labor exploitation that permeate our cultures, offering an alternative paradigm that uplifts longevity, purposefulness, and self-expression. Further, mending can serve as a model for something far more potent than purely the repair of clothing: it also offers us a model for the repair of relationships and the reparation of communities.

cɔʃ

Mending, Memory, History

Some might say that mending is an attempt to make brokenness whole again. But that doesn't seem to quite capture its purpose, in my opinion. I think it's a mistake to suggest that mending can ever achieve anything like completeness or perfection or wholeness. Not only are these things never really achieved, but I also don't think that's what mending has ever been about. And that's certainly never been the point of *visible* mending.

If this isn't the case, then what does mending have to teach us? What is the story that mending tells? What instructions do the passing of needle and thread and the patching of fabrics share? How might they shift our ideas and our habits?

Visible mending seems to be about something more important—and frankly, in my opinion, more interesting—than perfection or wholeness or completeness. It points to a different way of thinking, one that attunes itself to the flows of time.

Mending neither assumes an idyllic past nor promises a perfect future. But still it opens up the possibility of repair, the potentiality of transformation. In other words, mending is not about wholeness, though it may be an effort to realize *wholesomeness*. It creates beauty out of harm, but it does not suggest that harm is needed for beauty to exist in the first place.[2]

I'd like to suggest that the story that mending tells—that is, the lessons taught to us by mending as a creative practice—is a story about remembering pasts. Mending neither erases the past nor glorifies it, even as it endeavors to transform the present.

Here's my argument in two sentences: *Mending remembers. Remembering mends.*

Or, to put it slightly differently, *mending is re-membering.*

⟡

Mending Remembers;
Remembering Mends

In a way, mending has quite a lot to do with history. I don't simply mean that it's a practice that was far more prevalent in the past than it is now: that's obviously true, but it's not my angle here. Rather, I mean that mending has everything to do with *memory*.

Mending is an act of remembering. And *remembering is always a political act.*

To mend is to attend to the snags and snares of the past by seeking their repair in the present. Without this attention to evident harm, mending would not be possible.

If you think about it, the culture of the United States broadly can be characterized by an inclination to forget. Remembering is not something our society—at least in its whitest sectors—often encourages. By "remembering" I mean not the memorializing of nationalistic pursuits so much as the brutally honest recollection of the past, including all its woes, harms, traumas, and more. Remembering with honesty suggests we must not idolize or glamorize an imagined past.

Generally speaking, popular US culture not only exhibits a tendency to forget, but, worse, it seems to exhibit *a need to forget.* And that's not happenstance. But why?

Consider what you were likely taught—or, really, *weren't* taught—about US history. How much did you learn about the Tulsa race massacre? How much time was spent covering the Trail of Tears—that is, the forced displacement of sixty thousand indigenous persons, resulting in more than ten thousand deaths? When did you first discover that Laos is the most bombed nation on this planet due to the United States' secret war that lasted nearly a decade (1964–1973)? Did you know that the United States endorsed, funded, and directly supported authoritarian regimes in Argentina, Bolivia, Brazil, Ecuador, Guatemala, Haiti, and Nicaragua, not to mention others? How about in 1985, when Philadelphia police fire-bombed Black radical activists?

The United States' enactment of violence—particularly on nonwhite bodies—is overwhelming and abhorrent. That these legacies rarely occupy the majority of the United States' attention is not accidental. And this is because *to remember means to be responsible.* It is easier to forget, and forgetting absolves of any need to seek repair or realize justice. The historical amnesia that is endemic to the United States is not a coincidence.

Theologian and activist Jim Wallis notes that the most controversial statement he's ever written was not about abortion, queerness, or militarism but, rather, was simply about US history: "The United States of America was established as a white society, founded upon the near genocide of another race and then the enslavement of yet another."[3] Regardless of intention or motivation, this is simply a statement of the facts about the founding of this particular nation-state. How else are you supposed to tell this story? To tell the story any other way would be a farce, if not a lie. So why would this statement be controversial? It's what happened, regardless of whether one wishes that weren't the case. So why aren't "we"—by which I mean those of us who have benefited from these histories—encouraged to practice this sort of remembering?

I would like to suggest that the historical amnesia pervading the United States is, if nothing else, an attempt to avoid accountability. Or let me be more forthright: The historical amnesia that is prevalent among those who have long benefited from the status quo (i.e., *generally* those who are white, male, documented, educated, wealthy, straight, etc.) is an attempt to avoid being held accountable. To fail to remember that those who benefit from the status quo do so at the expense of the marginalized (i.e., *generally* those who are Black, Brown, feminine, undocumented, uneducated, poor, queer, etc.) absolves the privileged of their complicity.

Remembering is the first step, I think, to being in solidarity. It's the first step toward accountability.

Remembering necessitates keenly attending to not merely the question of *what*—as in, "What happened?"—but also the questions of *who*:

- *Who* benefited from the status quo during the moment in question?
- *Who* was excluded from or marginalized by the status quo "back then"?
- How did that moment come to shape *our* lives today?
- *Who* benefits from the status quo now?
- And *who* is disenfranchised by things as they currently stand?

As soon as these questions are asked, conversations about accountability and solidarity can follow. As womanist theologian M. Shawn Copeland argues, "Solidarity begins in *anamnesis*—the intentional remembering of the dead, exploited, despised victims of history."[4]

Thus, it bears repeating: *remembering is always a political act.*

Now, consider the various and variously successful attempts by political conservatives to manipulate history textbooks in the United States, sometimes requiring presenting "both sides" of an event as similarly "credible" and sometimes outright outlawing discussions about matters like chattel slavery, internment camps, US imperialism abroad, and more. This is not "forgetting" so much as it is, in Copeland's words, "repressive erasure."[5]

Regardless of intention, the consequence is the same: to fail to remember histories is to evade accountability.

Perhaps we can note that to be white is, in many ways, to be *not forced to remember*. To be white is to be *not constantly confronted* with the past atrocities committed by those of a similar complexion. Whiteness and its attendant privileges necessitate forgetting.

This sort of racial and political amnesia insulates whiteness from the cruelties that it has caused or been complicit in. Forgetting is easier when the alternative means being held accountable.

Those who benefit from the structures of white supremacy, misogyny, heterosexism, and the like—of which I am very much a part—possess a responsibility for transforming the cultures and systems that persist. As Wallis says, "To benefit from oppression is to be responsible for changing it."[6]

Crucially, responsibility is *not* the same as culpability. That I benefit from a particular system while others are marginalized by that same system does not mean that I am "guilty," per se. I, personally, did not create this system. But that does not negate the fact that *I am* complicit in it. And, thus, I have a responsibility *to* the harms caused by this system.

As peace advocate Rabbi Abraham Joshua Heschel wrote, "We must continue to remind ourselves that in a free society all are involved in what some are doing. *Some are guilty, all are responsible.*"[7] I did not cause the past, but I have inherited its outcomes and consequences; I am not guilty because of it (that is, I'm not "responsible for" causing it), but, upon recognizing it through remembrance, I am tasked with being responsible *to* it. And none of this diminishes the need to hold accountable those who are indeed *responsible for* it.

Thus, remembering is not a matter of suggesting that one is responsible *for* something, but it *does* mean that one is responsible *to* it. That I did not cause something does not mean that I don't continue to benefit from its legacies. That's why privilege need not mean that one's life has been easy or that one hasn't indeed worked hard. Rather, privilege means that, perhaps, there have been fewer obstacles in one's way. That the world does not actively work against me and that the legacies of the past do not routinely inhibit my flourishing—*that's* what privilege means.

Hence, the form of remembering that mending instills is not

about a fanciful memory of an Edenic past; rather, it's a reckoning with the fact that the façades of unity, freedom, possibility, and beyond were not always equitably available to all who wished for such things. It's not the exaltation of the past, for the exaltation of any past is only possible if one neglects, overlooks, or outright ignores those who did not benefit from the status quo—which has always been the case. There can be no forgetting of the past if we wish to remain committed to not replicating it.

So, what does mending have to teach about any of this? How might it help us respond to the brutal histories remembered?

To mend is to recognize harm and to toil to refurbish it by neither glossing over the damage incurred nor giving up entirely on the possibility of repair. Hence, mending is not an effort to make something great again—as if one could remember something as "great *again*" when it, in fact, never was or has been great to the dispossessed, marginalized, downtrodden, or oppressed. To the contrary, memory illustrates the vital importance of reparation. Reparation does not—indeed cannot—change the past; it does, however, *recognize* it. As James Baldwin rightly contended, "Not everything that is faced can be changed, but nothing can be changed until it is faced."[8] Recognition entails responsibility to repair.

Any time we mend, a mark remains; a scar persists. There'll always be a trace of what occurred. The story becomes threaded into the cloth.

I actually think that this is part of the allure of mending: *the visibility of history*. Mending tells a story—a story that refuses to hide that which has created the present. It reminds of what has led to this moment: snags, comforts, toils, warmth, neglect, care, hazards, and all else. Mending states it plain, you could say.

Mending suggests that things can be otherwise but that we can only make them otherwise by first recognizing damage. It demands that we tend to wounds, becoming present to the griefs of harm and the world that caused them. Yet it does not purport to erase those instances of harm; it cares for them, carefully stitching and thoughtfully patching. While they don't disappear, we are reminded that they can be made anew—tenderly.

Mending functions as a visualized *reclamation*: the snags, tears, and tatters of our histories must not be their end. They will not be that which defines the garment or the wearer, though they remain deeply relevant to their stories. To reclaim is to take back; it's a refusal to allow externally imposed conditions or projections to serve as defining characteristics. Again, mending is not an idolization of suffering, abuse, or tragedy. No one wishes for their textiles to be torn, tattered, or otherwise distressed. Mending is but the response to harm through tender care, serving as a tactile remembrance of history. This reclamation is, therefore, also resistance: resistance to an economy of waste (under the guise of efficiency) and a culture of consumerism (behind the façade of fashion).

But, even as mending is a form of reclaiming histories, it is also and simultaneously characterized by a relinquishing of control, in a sense. We can neither undo the past event that led to the need to mend nor can we turn a garment into something it's simply not. Mending is relational: we can only ever work in concert with the garment before us. The constraints, demands, and needs of the fabric—its thickness, flow, composition, style, weave, and so on—require that the mender *notice*. The mender cannot force their desires on the textile willy-nilly, lest they manipulate it in ways that are forced and contrived.

The real reparation of trauma occurs only if one listens to, understands, and fulfills the needs articulated—regardless of the sewer's interests or expertise. The mender cannot know better than the fabric does. It is the directly impacted alone who can lay claim to what is needed.

Repair is only ever possible *if in right relationship*—with fabric, with community.

In a climate-changed world, the necessity to listen to the least of these—to hear the cry of the poor and the cry of the Earth for the sake of repair—has never been greater.

☙

Practice Sacred Remembering

At the end of the street I live on, at the edge of a small park, stands the stump of a once-massive catalpa tree. I didn't know the tree, as I only recently moved to the area. But those who did tell stories of the home it provided, respite from overwhelming summer heat and habitat to the critters that scurry through and soar over this neighborhood.

Compared to the houses nearby, this catalpa was ancient. Its memory precedes any of us who currently inhabit the spaces near it, yet it was cut down without warning a handful of years ago. Something about safety, the economy, power lines, and other excuses. Routine maintenance and fire hazards. Typical. So the story often goes. Of course, the only possible solution imaginable to any of these contrived concerns was to decimate life. Whatever the *intent* was, it's diminished by the *impact* of the ravaging of the tree. No creative solutions to these human-caused problems—only quick fixes and the further problems that they generate.

In front of the stump today stands a hand-painted sign, now somewhat worn by the shifting seasons and the weather they bring. Pastel colors line aged wood, standing at a bit of a slant now. But the words scrawled across it are still clear:

Practice Sacred Remembering

The sign serves as a memorial of mourning for the tree, a public display of grief in response to environmental destruction so commonplace these days that it's hard not to become numb to it.

A local artist-activist, Lyric Morris-Latchaw, created the sign as *both* an act of remembrance *and* a denouncement of the systemic destruction that so often flies under the auspices of technology, development, and progress. The sign invites the viewer to witness to traumas of not just environmental degradation but *desecration*. In other words, it's a reminder that, as agrarian poet Wendell Berry contends, "There are no sacred and unsacred places; there are only sacred and *desecrated* places."[9]

These days, the sign is kind of hard to read—not because of the fading of paint but because, somehow, the catalpa has persisted. Out of the severed trunk, new limbs—many of them!—have shot forth. The catalpa "coppiced," which is the term used to describe the process of new growth emerging from a cut stump. In a way, this coppicing is a form of mending: reckoning with the scars of the past yet seeking creative opportunities for growth nevertheless. This doesn't always happen, but it can.

I have no doubt that the cycle will continue: the city and power company will return with their chainsaws to fell the catalpa—maybe soon. Yet there will be those—human, vegetal, and more—who continue to resist this desecration. And resist they will, only because they first choose to *remember*. Re-membering ourselves to this great tree, to the great tree of life, this neighborhood will persist—imperfectly but faithfully.

Practice sacred remembering. When we do, we stitch together our lives.

∽

How to Darn a Sock
(In Less Than Five Minutes)

❧

1. You should probably wash the sock if you haven't already. It's not necessary, I guess, but it might help make the experience a bit more pleasant. But to each their own.

2. Decide if you want to repair the sock inside out or not. Repairing it inside out means that it'll look "nicer" when worn. But repairing it inside out might also make it less comfortable because the stitching will be primarily on the inside. (Personally, I've never darned a sock inside out. What good is a sock if it's uncomfortable?)

3. Find a round object that you can put inside the sock to stretch it out a bit (to mimic your foot). Many people use a lightbulb or a tennis ball or something like that. It'll make the process much easier to have something in there. Trust me.

4. Get a needle and thread. Obviously.

5. Thread the needle. (*Optional step:* Curse out of frustration as much or as little as your ethics allow.)

6. Tie a knot on the end of your thread. Maybe a couple. Nothing fancy. Just something to stop the thread from sliding through at the end.

7. Insert the needle through the sock near the edge of the hole. If you're repairing it right-side out, start from the inside so that the knot you just tied is on the inside of the sock. (Honestly, you can do it the opposite way and leave

the knot on the outside, too. No one is going to see it but you. It doesn't matter. Do as you please.)

Now, it becomes a "choose your own adventure" sort of thing!

The "proper" way:	The "easy" way:
Make a grid of lines by passing the thread over and under the fabric. Allow the thread to cross the hole when you pass through that area. Your goal is to make a small square of little parallel lines. It should be one centimeter bigger than the hole on each of the sides. Roughly. It's just a sock.	Pass the needle and thread across the hole. There's no need to get fancy with it. You're just trying to close a hole.
Then do the same thing but perpendicular! Make another set of lines that are perpendicular to the ones you just did, again creating a small square that'll now look sort of like a checkerboard. Finish the stitch with a knot. You can do this by leaving a small loop, passing the needle through, and pulling tight.	Do what you need to do to close up the hole and keep those feet warm. If the hole is so big that when you do this it gets really bunched up or creased or something like that, then maybe it's worth doing it the "proper" way.
	Otherwise, just close up the hole with your thread. Then tie a finishing knot that'll keep your work from coming undone. Voilà.

Baking

Bread Alone

If I'm being honest, sometimes I wonder if—maybe, possibly—Jesus was wrong about one thing: that whole "man shall not live by bread alone" business. Sometimes I like to test this. Man shall not live by bread alone? Watch me.

Bread is remarkable. I love bread. There's beauty in its simplicity: flour, water, yeast, and salt. That's all you need. And frankly, depending on the type of bread you're going for—say, unleavened or unsalted—even the yeast and salt may not be necessary. Still, four mere ingredients yield one of humanity's most ingenious and, indeed, delicious creations.

Not everyone loves bread, I know. And not everyone can eat glutinous bread, I'm aware (and I'm sorry). But I'm not sure I've ever encountered someone who actively hates it. Can you imagine? You're at a restaurant and overhear, "Bread? Are you kidding me? Who would *ever* consider eating that stuff?" Unthinkable.

And, for any reading this—particularly North Americans—who think by "bread" I mean mass-produced, plastic-suffocated, atrociously soft sandwich bread from a major grocery store chain, please don't. That's not the kind of bread I'm referring to. That's the antithesis of what I mean by bread. Ironically, this sort of sliced bread may actually be the worst thing since . . . sliced bread.

Crusty baguettes. Steaming pita. Floury ciabatta. Charred naan. Oily focaccia. *That* kind of bread. And, yes, some of these creations

135

might require a bit of sugar or tablespoon of yogurt or gallon of olive oil to create them, but, at their core, they're flour and water and yeast and salt, transformed by time and labor and heat, to become something profound—daresay, *magical.*

It's not inconsequential that "bread" is a stand-in for "food" and "sustenance," generally—at least in societies where bread is the staple foodstuff (as opposed to rice or cassava or potato or maize).

There are perhaps few culinary creations as pivotal to human history as bread. Every culture seems to have some form of it, and relatively new evidence suggests that humans have been making bread for something like 14,400 years now.[1] If the stuff's been around effectively forever, does it still have anything to teach us here-now amid climate catastrophe?

What wisdom has a loaf?

℀

Bread-Baking

There are all kinds of baking—both in style and substance. One can bake in a tandoori oven or in an underground pit with hot coals; one can bake a meaty pie or a delicate meringue. Baking is quite an amorphous practice that can produce foodstuffs that cover the cultural expanses of culinary ingenuity.

I want to focus in this chapter on baking yeasted, wheaten bread. It's perhaps one of the simplest things to make, but simple does not mean easy here. I'm about a decade out from baking my first loaves, and I'm still no less mystified by the process now than I was then.

The variables for bread are few, but the complexity of the results they can produce—good and ill—are multitudinous.

Ingredients. Time. Temperature. Method. Each of these variables can be broken down into nearly limitless subcategories, even with a straightforward four-ingredient bread.

Ingredients:

- Flour: amount, type, moisture, granularity, protein content, absorption capacity, enzyme activity, etc.
- Water: amount, pH, hardness, salinity, etc.
- Salt: amount, type, granularity, surface area, etc.
- Yeast: amount, type, activity level, activation process, etc.

Time:

- Time allotted (or not!) for autolysis, mixing, kneading, folding, fermenting, shaping, proofing, baking, resting, etc.

Temperature:

- Temperature of ingredients, preparation environment, fermentation environment, oven, etc.

Method:

- Methods used (or not!) for autolysis, mixing, kneading, folding, fermenting, shaping, proofing, scoring, baking, resting, etc.
- Implements used (or not!) to measure, mix, rest, proof, shape, score, bake, store, etc.

If you really want to get into the weeds with baking a simple four-ingredient bread, you can. I have—maybe a bit obsessively.

But frankly, if you follow very basic principles, what comes out of the oven is always, inevitably, an edible and delicious loaf: Mix the ingredients to ensure that they're evenly distributed. Build tension in the dough to allow it to hold some sort of shape and not turn into a big, formless blob. Allow the dough to ferment (aka "rise").

Shape the dough into a loaf or place it in a vessel (e.g., a loaf pan) that will give it a shape. Bake it until cooked through. That's it.

Yeah, maybe the crumb ends up a bit tight, the crust is denser than you would have hoped, the rise was odd and irregular, or something like that. It'll still beat Wonder Bread, I can assure you that.

I find the complexity of the simple in bread baking utterly alluring. And, at times, frustrating.

∽

Jesus seemed quite fond of bread.

I mean, the central symbol of remembrance of the child-from-Bethlehem-turned-provocateur-in-Jerusalem is bread. "Then he took a loaf of bread, and when he had given thanks he broke it and gave it to them."

Aside from baptism, the Eucharist is perhaps the central-most sacramental ritual of Christianity. Bread becomes the body of Jesus the Christ in some capacity. And, yeah, denominations debate what is meant by "becomes" the body, never mind what kind of bread should be used, how to consume it, who can consecrate it, who can receive it, and all that. But, at its core, this ritual is effectively *impossible without bread.*

Consider the ecological dimensions of this practice for a moment. I ask you this:

If the bread has been made of wheat that's been sprayed with herbicides, pesticides, and fungicides, killing countless beings in the process; and if that wheat was fertilized with synthetic nitrogen fixers, whose runoff created oceanic dead zones; and if the bread was baked in a factory whose workers were made to toil in hellish conditions only to be paid an unlivable wage; and if the bread was packaged in an unrecyclable plastic bag that will not break down for at least twenty years; and if the bread was trucked across the country, thereby emitting untold amounts of carbon dioxide . . . is that still the body of Christ?

What have we done to the body of Christ?

Might it be the case that this act has become too toxic, too unjust, too damaging, too wasteful, too complicit to be holy? Has the sacred been profaned irreparably?[2]

Even if you still consider receiving the Eucharist with bread that has inflicted violence on land, water, air, and bodies as a holy act, these questions must, at least, make you pause. If this book has been an effort to draw attention to the ways in which theology and ecology are inseparably woven together, then I would argue that these particular queries about the Eucharist can serve as a gateway for Christian communities to consider their responsibility to seeking environmental justice. Even now. Even if it's too late.

But back to bread.

Even prior to "that fateful night," bread was at the core of Jesus's ministerial imagination and praxis: stories abound about his feeding of large crowds, and the parable-text we call the Gospel of John describes Jesus making a rather oddly wheaten claim: "I am the bread of life." We could spend the entire chapter exploring these vignettes, asking what precisely a "miracle" is or whether it's interpretatively appropriate to translate it as, "I am the rice of life," for East Asian contexts (among others).

Instead, I want to focus on something a bit more mundane: a strange story about a woman and dough.

In the Gospels we call Matthew and Luke, there's an odd, almost standalone passage: "And again [Jesus] said, 'To what should I compare the kingdom of God? It is like yeast that a woman took and mixed in with three measures of flour until all of it was leavened'" (Luke 13:20–21).[3]

Huh?

What an odd parable. It's so short, it almost seems cryptic. And interpreters of this text have been forever trying to uncover some sort of hidden meaning in each of the symbols. Church father Jerome suggests that the three measures of flour are indicative of "spirit, soul, and body"; Augustine thinks that the woman is a stand-in for "Wisdom"; John Chrysostom argued that the leaven is symbolic for the disciples.[4] Might it be simpler than that, though? Why make it so complicated?

What if Jesus was actually just talking about flour, yeast, and faithful labor? Let's see.

First off, can't the woman just be a woman? Jesus was always transgressing the status quo of his culture by interacting with not only women but "unrighteous" women. The Gospels are clear that there were women who were followers—daresay disciples—of Jesus. So, why must she be some sort of mythical wise-woman?

And none of this even begins to consider the fact that there is no Christianity without the faithful witness of women: there is no story of the resurrection without the persistence of women who took it upon themselves to care for and anoint the corpse of Jesus. Yes, the four canonical Gospels differ when it comes to who actually went to the tomb (just as they differ in naming the so-called twelve disciples), but all are clear that this happened only because of women. There is no story of the resurrection without women. There is no Christianity without women. Tell me again why the church cannot rid itself of its enduring patriarchal structure.[5] But perhaps I digress.

Second, what if the flour is just flour and the yeast is just yeast? And, by communing with them through faithful labor—modeled often by women—might we not only learn something of the "kingdom of God" but also participate in ushering it into our world here-now? How might bread baking be a radical act of making Earth just ever so slightly more heavenly?

The kingdom of God is like fermenting dough. What ever could that mean?

I think we've much to learn from yeast.

Surely, the woman who mixed the dough was not using commercially made, store-bought yeast. That is a thing of the industrial era and since. The leaven of her moment would have been wild, meaning naturally occurring yeasts that had been collected and cared for as a catalyst for baking (as well as brewing).

Yeast is everywhere. It's in fruits and flowers and seaweed and humans.

Yeast floats through the air all around us. This is why a sourdough starter culture can be made with just flour and water. When you mix the two and leave it open to the air, yeast will make its way into the mixture. By feeding the mixture with additional flour and water, the yeast culture multiplies as it converts carbohydrates to alcohol and carbon dioxide.

In all leavened bread, yeast functions to produce carbon dioxide, which allows the dough to rise while both fermenting and baking. And in so-called sourdoughs, the production of alcohol contributes to flavor—though its sourness is more so due to another crucial microorganism, lactic acid bacteria.

There's a kind of subversive and even enchanting nature to yeast. It's everywhere. You don't have to go buy it. You don't get to control it. You simply create conditions in which it can be grown, fed, nurtured. If you mix it, they will come.

Okay. Yeah. Yeast is cool. It's all over the place. But, somehow, this is supposed to teach us something about the kingdom of God?

Yes, and no. The text reads, "[The kingdom of God] is like yeast that a woman took and mixed in with three measures of flour until all of it was leavened." The kingdom of God is like yeast—but only with respect to its interplay and interrelations with both the woman and the flour. Yeast is everywhere, but it must be given the conditions in which it can thrive. The catalyst that is yeast matters not without a context in which it can flourish. And that context—the mixture of flour and water—does not just fall out of the sky. Leavened bread is not possible without yeast, but neither is it possible without faithful human labor—milling wheat, mixing dough, and so on.

Human and yeast in this kingdom serve each other as collaborators. They co-labor in symbiosis.

This kingdom is a *kindom*—and not solely of humans. This kindom is not a thing, object, or even place. It's relationality, companionship, collaboration. The kindom described in this terse parable is created through the seeking of right relationship—not perfect orthodoxy. It is the enactment of tender care, a loving-kindness that seeks to nurture and nourish. And the faithful work of compassion is never universal or selfsame; it is dependent on conditions, relationship, resources. In other words, it is attuned to the needs of the context, the moment, the place. It pays attention to its environs, to the behaviors of dough and the heat of the oven.

The kindom of God is thus everywhere and nowhere. It manifests not out of happenstance so much as out of cultivating the conditions in which it grows: namely, in *love*.

∽

Yeast and Change

What I find to be so subversive about yeast is the challenge it poses to our conceptions of change-making. It is often assumed that to make hopeful repair in the world means continued "progress" through incremental reforms, increasing growth, yield, efficiency, and the like. But, if the vector of these changes is pointed in the wrong direction, or if the results sought are undergirded by harmful logics, such change is bound to backfire, which is what we now see in this age of climate catastrophe: limitless capitalistic growth has led to the destruction of our ecosystems, insatiable desire for maximum efficiency of our fields has stripped our topsoil bare, and so on.

Rarely is the most efficient method the most loving. Efficiency typically excises aspects of a relationship in order to force a desired result, regardless of the harm caused along the way. The ends are made to justify the means. For example, the most "efficient" way to use my time as a teacher is to treat all students as having the same needs, to focus on grades rather than education, to streamline my courses with standardized tests that can be assessed with scantrons, to maintain strict deadlines with harsh punishments, and so forth. But whom does this efficiency serve—but me? Surely not first-generation college students trying to navigate the system of higher education, nor those whose creativity does not shine in rote tasks, nor those who are genuinely curious about theological concerns, nor those looking for mentorship in their vocational discernment, nor those who encounter grief mid-semester and struggle to submit their work "on time."

The same is true of bread. The most efficient way to make bread does not yield the most delicious bread. Not in the least. And do please tell me about how it might go for you if you attempted to be more efficient at love. That partner, that friend, that coworker, that family member would get reduced to a bunch of boxes to check: "Yep, did this. Mhmm, fulfilled that. Oh, and I even get to check this other box from last week! Looks like I'm all squared away. Love? Done. Accomplished. Next!"

Yeast upends our paradigms. If growth is possible, it is only through collaboration. Yet there is such a thing as too much growth. When a dough ferments too long—when it over-proofs, as bakers would say—something wild happens. It not only begins to deflate, losing the air buildup in the rising process, but it almost immediately gets *incredibly* sticky. It turns to a gluey mess. It's pretty much impossible to work with, unless you do something drastic like add heaps of flour to it.

And yet our economic theories seem to suggest that infinite growth is possible on a planet with finite resources.

∽

Hope and Leaven

If hope is not to be had so much as made, as I've attempted to argue in this book, then it must also be said that hope is not made by humans alone. Hope is not strictly a human effort.

To enact hope is to seek communion with soil and wheat and yeast—all of whom are our neighbors. Hope, if anything at all, requires our partnering with the more-than-human world and the divine spirit by and through whom our loving-hope flows.

Co-laboring with yeast requires our attention to the conditions of our environment and time. Living in a climate-changed world demands the very same.

The repair that must be sought presently is neither incremental nor reformist, because the narratives that have led us to the edge of collapse have been built on foundational logics that are neither good nor sustainable. The narratives of "progress" so often accompanying our cultural paradigms assume that they're pointed in the right direction. Clearly, they're not.

The repair that must be sought can be nothing short of *revolutionary*. It will mean making good trouble and flipping the tables of the money changers. But the radical change that's needed may not always be so apparent or in-your-face. It might at times be quieter, slower, gentler—kind of like the gentle kneading from Jesus's parable.

What better metaphor for the spirit-filled kindom so sought by Jesus than yeast? A potentiality that flows through all corners, which can be harnessed with tender care. Only in loving do we embrace and embolden this spirit.

To what shall we compare the kindom of God? It is like harnessing the potency of each moment: the opportunity to practice a love that seeks to mend broken webs of ecology, to hold accountable exploiters of beings and bioregions, and to embrace the uncertainty that this love, itself, may not succeed.

But it is good, and, thus, we are tasked with this question: Will we continue to mix and bake in service of a world of such radical equity and tenderness that it can go by no other name than the kingdom of God?

What else can we do but embrace the uncertainty and live into the mystery of faith? What else can we do but mix and knead and bake and break bread—together?

In so doing, we witness to a world that could be otherwise. Maybe we won't achieve that world. Maybe we will. But our witness is not predicated on success. It may work. It may fall flat. Regardless, it remains good.

Our witness is simply to be leaven to a world that has been toxified by greed, corrupted by capital, desertified by misogyny, and deforested by xenophobia.

Our witness is to toil in faith, maybe flipping tables along the way—even if it's too late.

Starting a Sourdough Starter

❦

Starting a sourdough culture (or starter) is quite simple. All you need are flour, water, a container of some sort, and a few days.

Before you get started, it's helpful to know some basic principles:

- Your mixture will always be a 1:1 ratio of flour to water. It doesn't matter how much you use so long as the ratio is correct. If you want a number to go by, I find 50g (or ~1.75oz) of each to be a good amount to work with if I'm not baking very regularly.
- Your culture will be more active in warmer areas of your home—say, seventy-five to eighty degrees Fahrenheit. If you don't have warm spots in your home, don't worry. It'll still work. The culture will just be a bit slower to rise.
- Once the culture is active, you will want to feed it once a day, or if you keep it in your refrigerator, once a week. If you mess this up, that's okay. Yeast is resilient. I've left mine on the counter for a week without feeding and didn't manage to kill it. And I've left it in the refrigerator for two months without feeding it, and it was still fine. Just know that it generally should be fed at this rate when possible.

To begin, do the following:

1. Simply mix equal parts flour and water in a container of some sort (e.g., canning jar). I find a chopstick helpful for mixing it up. Let it sit for two or so hours uncovered. Then cover it.

2. The following day, roughly 24 hours later, remove about 80 percent of your mixture. I recommend using this "discard" in other baking recipes (just look up "sourdough discard recipes"). Then add equal parts flour and water to the jar with the remaining starter.

3. The following day, repeat the previous step by removing 80 percent of the starter and then adding equal parts flour and water. This is what feeding the starter means. You might begin to notice some bubbles in the culture, which is what you're looking for.

4. Continue this process for a few days. By the fifth day your culture should be fairly active, meaning that it's ready for use. You will know it's ready to use when it doubles in size a handful of hours after mixing.

5. Once active, you simply need to feed it once a day (countertop) or once a week (refrigerator). Just know that, if you keep it in the refrigerator, you'll want to remove it a day prior to any planned baking, allowing it to increase its activity.

An active starter can be shared easily. What you remove can simply be placed in a different jar, fed, and gifted to others.

Find a recipe and experiment. You might end up baking a few loaves that look more like discuses than bread. That's okay. Turn them into breadcrumbs or croutons. Nothing needs to be wasted. Eventually—or maybe even right away—you'll bake a loaf that will astound you.

Take, eat.

Closing

Hope Doesn't Exist

Hope doesn't exist. Not on its own. Not in the abstract. Not as concept or emotion. It's not an object, thing, entity.

Hope *insists*, which is to say that *hope is the insistence that the world be made otherwise.*

Hope is praxis, is work, is discipline. Hope is woven.

Hope is a horizon of possibility. We never arrive at this horizon, yet it permeates our faithful acts all the same. It lures us beyond what "is" toward what *may yet be*. It is the enactment of "that which will have had to happen."[1] Not in "the future." Not "tomorrow." Not "soon." Not even "today." But *now*. Always, only, ever, *now*.

And, if hope is stitched—as incitement and allure—through the contours of our lives, we find ourselves knit into community with place and people, with context and critter.

By making hope, we participate in divine creativity and holy repair. It is the work of faith, and it is faithful even if it "fails."

Hope is communal.

Hope is communion.

Hope is the practice of resurrection.

Notes

Opening

[1]Willie Jennings, "Hope as a Discipline," *The Veritas Forum,* November 11, 2020, https://youtu.be/o-P1l3_FHSY.

[2]Jennings.

[3]Mitri Raheb, *Faith in the Face of Empire: The Bible through Palestinian Eyes* (Maryknoll, NY: Orbis Books, 2014), 130.

[4]The Red Nation, *The Red Deal: Indigenous Action to Save Our Earth* (Brooklyn, NY: Commons Notions, 2021), 32.

[5]For example, see Tim Jackson, *Post-Growth: Life after Capitalism* (Cambridge: Polity Press, 2021); Drew Pendergrass and Troy Vettese, *Half-Earth Socialism: A Plan to Save the Future from Extinction, Climate Change and Pandemics* (New York: Verso Books, 2022); Red Nation, *Red Deal*; and others.

[6]Gary Paul Nabhan, *The Cultures of Habitat: On Nature, Culture and Story* (Washington, DC: Counterpoint, 1997), 319.

[7]See, for example, Elizabeth Kolbert, *The Sixth Extinction: An Unnatural History* (New York: Henry Holt, 2014).

[8]William R. Herzog II, *Parables as Subversive Speech: Jesus as Pedagogue of the Oppressed* (Louisville, KY: Westminster John Knox Press, 1994), 3.

[9]Some might argue that this parable isn't even a parable, in itself, as it is neither a simile or metaphor (as most parables are) but is instead an "example story." One argument to this end can be found in Marcus Mescher, *The Ethics of Encounter: Christian Neighbor Love as a Practice of Solidarity* (Maryknoll, NY: Orbis Books, 2020), 36. Even if this story does not neatly fit into the parameters of the strict definitions of a parable, its reception history and ongoing translatability for contemporary contexts suggests that—even if it does not qualify as a parable in Luke's Gospel—it *functions* as a parable today.

[10]Some scholars suggest that this strife is attributable to the destruction of the Samaritan temple at Mount Gerizim and the subsequent defilement of the Jewish temple at Jerusalem. For a helpful literary and historical excursus of the parable and, in particular, the strife between Jews and Samaritans, see Greg W. Forbes, *The God of Old: The Role of the Lukan Parables in the Purpose of Luke's Gospel* (Sheffield: Sheffield Academic Press, 2000), 55–71; for an alternative argument about one of the primary events contributing to this division, see Jonathan Bourgel, "The Destruction of the Samaritan Temple by John Hyrcanus: A Reconsideration," *Journal of Biblical Literature* 135, no. 3 (2016): 505–523.

[11]For more, see Bruce Metzger and Michael Coogan, eds., *The Oxford Companion to the Bible* (Oxford: Oxford University Press, 1993), 671–673.

[12]For an engaging discussion of this lesson from the perspective of the poor and through the lens of liberation theology, see Ernesto Cardenal, *The Gospel in Solentiname*, trans. Donald D. Walsh (Eugene, OR: Wipf and Stock, 2020), 331–336.

[13]My gratitude is owed to Dr. Traci West, teacher and mentor, for first introducing me to this reimagination of this idea.

[14]Mary Oliver, "The Summer Day," in *Devotions: The Selected Poems of Mary Oliver* (New York: Penguin Press, 2017), 316.

[15]"Didn't Know What I Was in For," Better Oblivion Community Center (Phoebe Bridgers and Conor Oberst), *Dead Oceans*, 2019.

Noticing

[1]Alfred North Whitehead, *Process and Reality: An Essay in Cosmology*, corrected ed., ed. David Ray Griffin and Donald Sherburne (New York: Free Press, 1978), 340.

[2]C. Robert Mesle, *Process-Relational Philosophy: An Introduction to Alfred North Whitehead* (West Conshohocken, PA: Templeton Foundation Press, 2008), 5.

[3]Tina M. Campt, *Listening to Images* (Durham, NC: Duke University Press, 2017), 17.

Birding

[1]Robin Wall Kimmerer, *Braiding Sweetgrass: Indigenous Wisdom, Scientific Knowledge, and the Teachings of Plants* (Minneapolis, MN: Milkweed Editions, 2013), 56.

[2]Kimmerer, 55.

[3]Kimmerer, 57.

[4]Thomas Berry, "The Meadow across the Creek," in *The Great Work: Our Way into the Future* (New York: Bell Tower, 1999), 16.

[5]Pauline Oliveros, *The Roots of the Moment* (New York: Drogue Press, 1998), 3.

[6]Pauline Oliveros, *Deep Listening: A Composer's Sound Practice* (New York: iUniverse, 2005), xxii (emphasis mine).

[7]Jenny Odell, *How to Do Nothing: Resisting the Attention Economy* (New York: Melville House, 2019), 7.

[8]Odell, 8.

[9]Odell, xi.

[10]Odell, xii.

[11]See Anna Lowenhaupt Tsing, *The Mushroom at the End of the World: On the Possibility of Life in Capitalist Ruins* (Princeton, NJ: Princeton University Press, 2015), 17–25.

[12]Odell, *How to Do Nothing*, 8.

[13]Terry Tempest Williams, *Erosion: Essays of Undoing* (New York: Sarah Crichton Books, 2019), 45.

[14]Whitehead, *Process and Reality*, 525.

[15]Odell, *How to Do Nothing*, xxiii.

[16]Walter Benjamin, *Selected Writings*, 4 vols., ed. Howard Eiland and Michael W. Jennings (Cambridge, MA: Harvard University Press, 2003), 4:397.

[17]Williams, *Erosion,* 46.

[18]See Pope Francis, *Laudato Si': On Care for Our Common Home*, Vatican.va, 2015.

Foraging

[1]For a theological extension of this phrase, see Catherine Keller, *On the Mystery: Discerning Divinity in Process* (Minneapolis, MN: Fortress Press, 2008).

[2]For an approachable and interactive description of the Doctrine of Discovery, including links to relevant papal bulls, among other resources, see "Doctrine of Discovery," *The Doctrine of Discovery Project*, 2024, https://doctrineofdiscovery.org/.

[3]Pope Alexander VI, *Inter caetera,* papal bull, May, 4, 1493.

[4]Pope Nicholas V, *Dum diversas,* papal bull, June 18, 1452; while it may appear on the surface that this papal bull was geographically bound,

its use—never mind its underlying theological justification of atrocious acts as such—was the justification for the enslavement of non-Christians and the subjugation of so-called non-Christian territories under the Catholic monarchy.

[5]For an excellent analysis of these matters, see Willie James Jennings, *The Christian Imagination: Theology and the Origins of Race* (New Haven, CT: Yale University Press, 2010).

[6]This is true even with a "negative rights" document like the Bill of Rights, which frames one's rights as the matters from which one is entitled to be free with respect to the government.

[7]Robin Wall Kimmerer, *Braiding Sweetgrass: Indigenous Wisdom, Scientific Knowledge, and the Teachings of Plants* (Minneapolis, MN: Milkweed Editions, 2013), 193.

[8]Kimmerer, 194.

[9]Abraham Joshua Heschel, *Abraham Joshua Heschel: Essential Writings,* ed. Susanna Heschel (Maryknoll, NY: Orbis Books, 2011), 57.

[10]Kimmerer, *Braiding Sweetgrass*, 190.

Composting

[1]The second creation story in Genesis (Gen. 2:4–3:24) refers to the divine by the name, Lord God (which differs from the name of the divine in Gen. 1:1–2:3), hence its use here.

[2]See René Descartes, *Meditations on First Philosophy,* 2nd ed., trans. John Cottingham (Cambridge: Cambridge University Press, 2017), 20–27.

[3]Octavia Butler, *Parable of the Sower* (New York: Grand Central Publishing, 1993), 3.

Gathering

[1]Kathryn Yusoff, *A Billion Black Anthropocenes or None* (Minneapolis: University of Minnesota Press, 2018), xiii.

[2]Yusoff, 12.

[3]Yusoff, 106.

[4]Auden Schendler, "Worrying about Your Carbon Footprint Is Exactly What Big Oil Wants You to Do," *New York Times,* August 31, 2021, https://www.nytimes.com/2021/08/31/opinion/climate-change-carbon-neutral.html.

[5]Jenny Odell, *How to Do Nothing: Resisting the Attention Economy* (New York: Melville House, 2019), xi.

[6]Robin Wall Kimmerer, *Braiding Sweetgrass: Indigenous Wisdom, Scientific Knowledge, and the Teachings of Plants* (Minneapolis, MN: Milkweed Editions, 2013), 239.

Seed-Saving

[1]Judy's kale is available for purchase through the praiseworthy seed-saving organization Truelove Seeds, here: "Judy's Siberian Kale," Truelove Seeds, accessed June 11, 2024, https://trueloveseeds.com/products/judys-siberian-kale?_pos=2&_sid=f427bab7f&_ss=r.

[2]On the ethical, gendered, and sociopolitical dimensions of GMO seeds and other related matters, see Vandana Shiva, *Biopiracy: The Plunder of Nature and Knowledge* (Berkeley, CA: North Atlantic Books, 2016).

[3]See, for example, Mateo Pimentel and Rebecca Monteleone, "A Privileged Bodymind: The Entanglement of Ableism and Capitalism," *International Journal of Economic Development* 12, no. 1 (2019): 63–81.

[4]Wendell Berry, *The Unsettling of America: Culture and Agriculture* (New York: Counterpoint Press, 1977), 35 (emphasis mine).

[5]For more on this idea in theoretical, theological, and political registers, see O'neil Van Horn, *On the Ground: Terrestrial Theopoetics and Planetary Politics* (New York: Fordham University Press, 2024).

[6]Thom Van Dooren, *Flight Ways: Life and Loss at the Edge of Extinction* (New York: Columbia University Press, 2016), 60–61.

[7]Kimmerer, *Braiding Sweetgrass*, 189–190.

Fermenting

[1]Sandor Ellix Katz, *Fermentation as Metaphor* (White River Junction, VT: Chelsea Green, 2020), 9.

[2]Katz, 12.

[3]Katz, 13–15 (emphasis mine).

[4]Katz, 17.

[5]Katz, 17–18.

[6]Katz, 16.

[7]For a feminist theological extension of this sort of claim, see the classic text by Elizabeth A. Johnson, *She Who Is: The Mystery of God in Feminist Theological Discourse* (New York: Crossroad, 1992).

[8]Katz, *Fermentation as Metaphor*, 4.

[9]Katz, 44–45.

[10]Ron Sender, Shai Fuchs, and Ron Milo, "Revised Estimates for the

Number of Human and Bacteria Cells in the Body," *PLOS Biology* 14, no. 8 (2016): e1002533, https://doi.org/10.1371/journal.pbio.1002533.

[11]Katz, *Fermentation as Metaphor,* 37.

[12]Katz, 44.

[13]Katz, 63.

[14]Katz, 49.

[15]Mercedes Villalba, *Manifiesto Ferviente* (Cali, Colombia: Calipso, 2019), 17, 19.

[16]Villalba, 21.

[17]Ralf Konietzka, Alyssa A. Goodman, Catherine Zucker, et al., "The Radcliffe Wave Is Oscillating," *Nature* 628 (2024): 62–65.

[18]Thomas Berry, "The Meadow across the Creek," in *The Great Work: Our Way into the Future* (New York: Bell Tower, 1999), 16.

[19]Kimmerer, *Braiding Sweetgrass,* 384.

Cycling

[1]Brendan Borrell, "The Bicycle Problem That Nearly Broke Mathematics," *Nature* 535 (2016): 338–341.

[2]J.P. Meijaard, Jim M. Papadopoulos, Andy Ruina, and A. L. Schwab, "Linearized Dynamics Equations for the Balance and Steer of a Bicycle: A Benchmark and Review," *Proceedings of the Royal Society A* 463 (2007): 1955–1982.

[3]J. D. G. Kooijman et al., "A Bicycle Can Be Self-Stable without Gyroscopic or Caster Effects," *Science* 332 (2011): 339–342.

[4]I'll use the terms "cycle," "bike," and "bicycle" almost interchangeably. "Cycle" is the most denotatively inclusive term to refer to the machines with wheels that we, humans, in some way power and ride about. It's intentionally ambiguous, though, as it doesn't suggest the exact form that the machine takes. Yet I'll also use "bike" and "bicycle," not to reference solely two-wheeled machines that can only be ridden by able-bodied persons; rather, I'll use them to mean the same thing as the intentionally ambiguous "cycle," simply because of the conversational and palatable nature of the terms (over against "cycle").

[5]Adrienne LaFrance, "How the Bicycle Paved the Way for Women's Rights," *The Atlantic,* June 26, 2014, https://www.theatlantic.com/technology/archive/2014/06/the-technology-craze-of-the-1890s-that-forever-changed-womens-rights/373535/.

[6]David J. C. MacKay, *Sustainable Energy: Without the Hot Air* (Cambridge, UK: UIT Cambridge Limited, 2009), 128.

[7]S. S. Wilson, "Bicycle Technology," *Scientific American* 228, no. 3 (March 1973): 81.

[8]Bruno Latour, *Down to Earth: Politics in the New Climatic Regime,* trans. Catherine Porter (Cambridge, MA: Polity Press, 2018), 70.

[9]Jonathan Masters and Will Merrow, "U.S. Aid to Israel in Four Charts," Council on Foreign Relations, May 31, 2024, https://www.cfr.org/article/us-aid-israel-four-charts.

[10]These figures are accurate as of the time this chapter was composed. See Jewish Institute for National Security of America (JINSA), "Read about U.S. Arms Transfers to Israel since Oct. 7," *New York Times,* July 25, 2024, https://www.nytimes.com/interactive/2024/07/25/us/jinsa-arms-transfer.html. For more on the controversial use of the MK-84 one-ton bombs, see John Ismay, "A Brief History of the 2,000-Pound Bombs Central to U.S.-Israeli Tensions," *New York Times,* May 11, 2024, https://www.nytimes.com/2024/05/11/us/israel-gaza-bombs.html.

[11]Cherice Bock, "Watershed Discipleship," in *An Ecotopian Lexicon,* ed. Matthew Schneider-Mayerson and Brent Ryan Bellamy (Minneapolis: University of Minnesota Press, 2019), 308.

[12]Bock, 308 (emphasis mine).

[13]Bock, 308.

[14]Hiroyuki Iseki and Matthew Tingstrom, "A New Approach for Bikeshed Analysis with Consideration of Topography, Street Connectivity, and Energy Consumption," *Computers, Environment and Urban Systems* 48 (November 2014): 166–77. What's more, as my dear colleague and historian Kathleen Smythe would remind, it's worth noting that cyclesheds often follow the arterial branches of a watershed. Bike paths can often be found alongside waterways, as waterways typically serve as a gradually sloped path that facilitates travel. Watersheds and cyclesheds are more intertwined than we might think at first glance.

[15]Carlos Moreno et al., "Introducing the '15-Minute City': Sustainability, Resilience and Place Identity in Future Post-Pandemic Cities," *Smart Cities* 4, no. 1 (2021): 93–111.

[16]For more, see Hannah Steinkopf-Frank, "Solarpunk Is Not about Pretty Aesthetics. It's about the End of Capitalism," *Vice,* September 2, 2021, https://www.vice.com/en/article/solarpunk-is-not-about-pretty-aesthetics-its-about-the-end-of-capitalism/.

[17]See Alexis Shotwell, *Against Purity: Living Ethically in Compromised Times* (Minneapolis: University of Minnesota Press, 2016).

[18]Of course, it's worth noting that none of what's proposed here is in

any way revolutionary or novel to those who dwell in places like Utrecht, Amsterdam, Copenhagen, Antwerp, and the like.

[19]Sam Robinson, "Why Are Runners Obsessed with the Pain Cave?" *Outside,* June 27, 2017, https://www.outsideonline.com/health/running/why-are-runners-obsessed-with-pain-cave/.

[20]Note: For the sake of ease of reading, I am citing the 1866 edition of *Gammer Gurton's Garland, or, The Nursery Parnassus: A Choice Collection of Pretty Songs and Verses for the Amusement of All Little Good Children Who Can Neither Read nor Run* (Glasgow: Hugh Hopkins, 1866), 29.

[21]Clifton Johnson, *What They Say in New England: A Book of Signs, Sayings, and Superstition* (Boston: Lee and Shepard, 1896), 144.

[22]Johnson, 144.

[23]R. I. M. Dunbar et al., "Performance of Music Elevates Pain Threshold and Positive Affect: Implications for the Evolutionary Function of Music," *Evolutionary Psychology* 10, no. 4 (2012): 688–702.

[24]For example, Emil Durkheim, *The Elementary Forms of Religious Life* (New York: Free Press, 1915); Barbara Ehrenreich, *Dancing in the Streets: A History of Collective Joy* (New York: Metropolitan, 2006); David Huron, "Is Music an Evolutionary Adaptation?" *Annals of the New York Academy of Sciences* 930, no. 1 (2001): 43–61; among many others.

Repairing

[1]Shannon Hall, "Exxon Knew About Climate Change almost 40 Years Ago," *Scientific American,* October 26, 2015, https://www.scientificamerican.com/article/exxon-knew-about-climate-change-almost-40-years-ago/.

Sowing

[1]David Abram, *Becoming Animal: An Earthly Cosmology* (New York: Vintage Books, 2011), 27 (emphasis mine).

[2]"Reports," The UN Intergovernmental Panel on Climate Change, 2024, https://www.ipcc.ch/reports/.

[3]David Wallace-Wells, *The Uninhabitable Earth: Life after Warming* (New York: Tim Duggan Books, 2019), 3.

[4]Jenny Odell, *Saving Time: Discovering a Life beyond the Clock* (New York: Random House, 2023), xxx.

[5]Odell, xviii.

[6]Hannah Arendt, *The Human Condition* (Chicago: University of Chicago Press, 1958), 190.

[7]Tina M. Campt, *Listening to Images* (Durham, NC: Duke University Press, 2017), 17.

[8]Catherine Keller, *On the Mystery: Discerning Divinity in Process* (Minneapolis, MN: Fortress Press, 2008), 17.

[9]Paul Tillich, *Dynamics of Faith* (New York: Harper, 1957), 1–2.

[10]Tillich, 20.

[11]Tillich, 9–10.

[12]Tillich, 21 (emphasis mine).

[13]Tillich, 25.

[14]Tillich, 120.

[15]Tillich, 117–118.

[16]Tillich, 20.

[17]Paul Tillich, *The Courage to Be* (New Haven, CT: Yale University Press, 1952), 155.

[18]For theological meditations emphasizing survival, resistance, and quality of life over against potentially abstract notions of salvation, see Delores Williams, *Sisters in the Wilderness: The Challenge of Womanist God-Talk* (Maryknoll, NY: Orbis Books,1993), esp. 19–26, 127–157; Monica A. Coleman, *Making a Way out of No Way: A Womanist Theology* (Minneapolis, MN: Fortress Press, 2008), esp. 11–84.

[19]Tillich, *Dynamics of Faith,* 116.

[20]Tillich, 48.

[21]Thomas Merton, *Thomas Merton: Essential Writings,* ed. Christine M. Bochen (Maryknoll, NY: Orbis Books, 2000), 135.

[22]Merton, 136.

[23]*Pirkei Avot* 2:16.

[24]Cristina Milesi et al., "A Strategy for Mapping and Modeling the Ecological Effects of US Lawns," *The International Society for Photogrammetry and Remote Sensing,* 2005, https://www.isprs.org/proceedings/XXXVI/8-W27/milesi.pdf.

Mending

[1]While the term "visible mending" is relatively new, increasing in popularity in the twenty-teens, communities have been visibly mending textiles in simple yet beautiful ways for countless ages, one of the most notable perhaps being the Japanese mending of *boro* (mended and patched textiles) known as *sashiko*. For a guide to *sashiko* for a Western audience, see Susan Briscoe, *The Ultimate Sashiko Sourcebook: Patterns, Projects, and Inspirations* (Exeter: David and Charles, 2005). For a historical excursus and historical analysis of the practice of sashiko on boro, see Yoshiko

Iwamoto Wada, "Boro no Bi: Beauty in Humility—Repaired Cotton Rags of Old Japan," *Textile Society of America Ninth Biennial Symposium* (2004), https://digitalcommons.unl.edu/cgi/viewcontent.cgi?article=14 58&context=tsaconf.

[2]Some psychologists call this phenomenon "posttraumatic growth" (PTG), which considers how some people grow in significant ways after experiencing trauma while also not condoning that which led to that trauma. My gratitude is owed to my dear friend and colleague Dr. Nathan Mather for providing this language and drawing this connection.

[3]Jim Wallis, *America's Original Sin: Racism, White Privilege, and the Bridge to a New America* (Grand Rapids: Brazos Press, 2016), 33.

[4]M. Shawn Copeland, *Enfleshing Freedom: Body, Race, and Being,* 2nd ed. (Minneapolis, MN: Fortress Press, 2023), 100.

[5]M. Shawn Copeland, "The Risk of Memory, The Cost of Forgetting," *Journal of the Black Catholic Theological Symposium* 9 (2016): 70.

[6]Wallis, *America's Original Sin,* 34–35.

[7]Abraham Joshua Heschel, "A Prayer for Peace," from *Moral Grandeur and Spiritual Audacity: Essays,* ed. Susannah Heschel (New York: Farrar, Straus and Giroux, 1996), 231.

[8]James Baldwin, "As Much Truth as One Can Bear: To Speak Out about the World as It Is, Says James Baldwin, Is the Writer's Job," *New York Times,* January 14, 1962. https://timesmachine.nytimes.com/times-machine/1962/01/14/118438007.html?pageNumber=120.

[9]See Bill Moyers, "Wendell Berry: Poet and Prophet," *HuffPost,* October 2, 2013, https://www.huffpost.com/entry/wendell-berry-poet-proph_b_4031836.

Baking

[1]Amaia Arranz-Otaegui et al., "Archaeobotanical Evidence Reveals the Origins of Bread 14,400 Years Ago in Northeastern Jordan," *Proceedings of the National Academy of Sciences* 115, no. 31 (July 31, 2018): 7925–7930.

[2]All credit is due to Dr. Laurel Kearns, my teacher and guide, for introducing me to these questions, this conflict, and thus this responsibility.

[3]The parallel iteration of this in Matthew can be found in Matthew 13:33.

[4]See Thomas Aquinas, *Catena aurea: Commentary on the Four Gospels, Collected out of the Works of the Fathers,* vol. 2: *St. Matthew* (Oxford: James Parker, 1874), 504–505.

[5]Some might protest these arguments by appealing to sparse verses in,

say, 1 Timothy. Those who might choose to make this case should consider how these are to be read in light of contrasting arguments made in, say, Galatians or 1 Corinthians or Romans. And this doesn't even begin to ask the critical questions about 1 Timothy's authorship, date, or similar. . . .

Closing

[1]Tina M. Campt, *Listening to Images* (Durham, NC: Duke University Press, 2017), 17.

Index